A VERY SPECIAL FAMILY

The House of Joseph Thomas Raad
Georgetown, S.C.
1895 – 2017

John Kenny

A VERY SPECIAL FAMILY
The House of Joseph Thomas Raad
Georgetown, S.C.

John Kenny

Copyright © 2017

All rights reserved.

Published in the United States by
CLASS
Publishing Division
P.O. Box 2884
Pawleys Island, SC 29585
www.ClassAtPawleys.com

In accordance with the U.S. Copyright Act of 1976, the scanning, uploading and electronic sharing of any part of this book without the permission of the publisher is unlawful piracy and theft of the author's intellectual property.
If you would like to use material from the book (other than for review purposes), prior written permission must be obtained by contacting the publisher.

ISBN 978-1-941069-71-4

CONTENTS

I Believe in You	v
Dedication	vi
Initial Research	vii
Prologue	x

SECTION 1 - INTRODUCTION AND HISTORY 1

Who Are the Lebanese?	2
Phoenicians, Lebanese, Americans	3
Historic Backdrop	5
Modern History of Lebanon	5
Emigration to Georgetown, South Carolina	7
Life in Georgetown, SC, as the Lebanese Arrived	8
The Lebanese Emigration	11
Lebanese Christians, Maronites and Roman Catholics	14
Lebanese/Irish Families of 1900 Become Model for Church Merger in 2017	22
A Timely Memoir	24
Georgetown 1800s to the Turn of the Century	27
Georgetown's Mayor at 1893 World's Fair in Chicago - A Marketing Mission	28
Challenges Faced by Lebanese who Came to America	31
The Centrality of Color in 1900 U.S. Immigration Law	32
Discrimination Among Immigrants	34

SECTION 2 - THE RAAD/JOSEPH FAMILY 37

The Parents and Their Proud 300-Year Heritage	39
The Initial Journey and Arrival	43
Coat of Arms	45
A Welcome Mat is Placed Out to Immigrants	49
Vignette: The One-Hundred-Year Trip	51
Raad/Joseph Family Reunions and the Tree	54

N. Joseph & Brother	60
Nicholas Raad Joseph and Thomas Raad Joseph	61
Nicholas Raad Joseph	63
Vignette: The Nicholas Joseph Family	64
Thomas Raad Joseph	71
Vignette: John Anthony Joseph	76
Vignette: Helen Joseph Walsh	79
Vignette: Zion Veronica Joseph Amann	85
Vignette: David Thomas Joseph	89
Vignette: Paul Joseph's Legacy - Lebanese Lakehouse	92
The Joseph Family Dental Dynasty	96
The Camden Dental Story, Drs. David and Paul Joseph, DDS	100
Vignette: Pauline Joseph Sottile - The Almost Nun and Her Immaculate Conception Twins	102
Shickory Raad Joseph	104
Vignette: Shickory Raad Joseph	106
Vignette: Dr. Arthur Joseph, DDS	109
Vignette: A Church Forms in the Wilderness	111
John Raad Joseph	113
John Raad Joseph	115
Vignette: Amelia Agnes Joseph Isaac	119
Vignette: Nellie Joseph Dorion	124
Vignette: Nellie Joseph Dorion	127
Vignette: Marie Joseph Franks	129
Vignette: Alfred Paul Joseph, Sr.	131
Vignette: Mary Louise Joseph - A Love Story for the Ages	138
The Remarkable Institution Called Thomas'	141
Dolly Raad-Awkar	150
EPILOGUE	153
A Final Vignette: July 4th at Jeddi's	155
ACKNOWLEDGMENTS	157
REFERENCES	158

I BELIEVE IN YOU by Kahlil Gibran

I believe in you, and I believe in your destiny.
I believe that you are contributors to this new civilization.
I believe that you have inherited from forefathers an ancient dream, a song, a prophecy, which can proudly lay as a gift of gratitude upon the lap of America.
I believe you can say to the founders of this great nation, "Here I am, a youth, young tree whose roots were plucked from the hills of Lebanon, yet I am deeply rooted here, and I would be fruitful."
And I believe that you can say to Abraham Lincoln, the blessed Jesus of Nazareth touched your lips when you spoke, and guided your hand when you wrote: and I shall uphold all that you have said and all that you have written.
I believe that you can say to Emerson and Whitman and James, "in my veins runs the blood of the poets and wise men of old, and it is my desire to come to you and receive, but I shall not come with empty hands."
I believe that even as your others came to this land to produce riches, you were born here to produce riches by intelligence, by labor.
And I believe that is in you to be good citizens.
And what is it to be a good citizen?
It is to acknowledge the other person's rights before asserting your own, but always to be conscious of your own.
It is to be free in thought and deed, but it is also to know that your freedom is subject to the other person's freedom.
It is to create the useful and the beautiful with your own hands, and to admire that others have created in love and with faith.
It is to produce wealth by labor and only by labor and to spend less than you have produced that your children may not be dependent on the state for support when you are no more.
It is to stand before the towers of New York, Washington, Chicago and San Francisco saying in your heart, "I am the descendant of a people that built Damascus, and Byblos and Tyre and Sidon and Antioch and now I am here to build with you and with a will."
It is to be proud of being an American, but it is also to be proud that your fathers and mothers came from a land upon which God laid his gracious hand and raised His messengers.
Young Americans of Syrian origin, I believe in you.

Kahlil Gibran addressed young Americans of Syrian/Lebanese origin in the first issue of *The Syrian World*, 1905 [23]

DEDICATION

This work is dedicated to two beautiful Lebanese American women, both named Mary Louise. One is my wife and one is my mother-in-law.

The first, my wife, introduced me to the special spice that is at the heart of the Lebanese people. It pervades their food, their speech, their way of life. It has a heat to it, but also a softness. It is strong yet subtle. Mary Lou is much like her dad who epitomized that strength.

The second was my mother-in-law who unraveled for me the depth of character of the Lebanese, the importance of family and a personal relationship with God. Right up until her death at age 93, she possessed a strength of spirit and mind and body to be truly envied.

Each in her own way helped me to understand why the Lebanese who came to Georgetown are a special family, who made it a better place.

I would note that, from hindsight, it seems prophetic that two things occurred when I arrived in Georgetown in the summer of 2011 to live permanently. The Joseph family held one of its 150-person-strong reunions, giving me a chance to savor the spice close up and to meet and greet the extended diaspora. Also, that summer, I awoke one day to find a proud old wooden fishing boat towed up on the rails in dry dock at the Fish House a block away, named Miss Louise II.

Little did I know when we moved to Georgetown to assist with the care for Mary Lou's mother how much she and the Lebanese community in town would become a part of my everyday life. I am better for it and so is Georgetown. It is they who have inspired me to write this.

John Kenny

INITIAL RESEARCH

My wife and I were living in Arlington, Virginia in the late 1990s while we worked in Washington, D.C. We had just returned from South Carolina and my first Raad/Joseph family reunion. It was that reunion that sparked my interest in this special family.

What I discovered was that a diaspora had occurred that stretched through the entire 20th century. Three million plus Lebanese had dispersed from the homeland that they had occupied for three centuries. Most of those who left Lebanon had emigrated to the Americas. The overwhelming majority had come to the United States. Their most famous migrant was the author and poet, Kahlil Gibran. It was he who, in 1925, penned his now famous Open Letter to the Lebanese Parliament and asked: "Are you a politician asking what your country can do for you or a zealous one asking what you can do for your country?" It was a powerful and prophetic question that foretold the longing of many in Lebanon, whose politicians had forsaken them and who felt compelled to migrate to countries where future politicians would respond properly to the question and the call. For those of us who grew up in America in the 1960s, it was John F. Kennedy in his 1961 Inaugural Address who would embrace Gibran's 40-year-old question and issue it as a challenge to a new generation of Americans and their politicians.

My research showed that the Raad/Joseph family had been living the Gibran-Kennedy ideal for more than one hundred years, here in America. They had decided there was a lot they could do for their adopted country!

While in Arlington, I found online a scholarly research paper that had been written by a fellow Virginian while a student at Clemson University in South Carolina. Elizabeth Virginia Whitaker had done extensive research as a Masters of Arts History candidate into the migration and assimilation of Lebanese families into Greenville, South Carolina in the early 1900s. The title of her 2006 thesis was: *From the Social Margins to the Center, Lebanese Families who Arrived in South Carolina Before 1950.* [46]

When I began thinking about writing an essay on the Lebanese in Georgetown, S.C., in December of 2010, I attempted to reach out to her both to compliment her on her work, and to see if she had done any further work in the four years since her submission. I learned that she had been living in nearby Alexandria, Va., about 10 minutes from my home in Arlington. I was saddened to learn that, at the young age of 51, Ms. Whitaker had died after a battle with cancer earlier that year. Her obituary indicated that she was working on "a book about Lebanese Christians in the South." [10] She wrote with passion and purpose, and her thesis bears out the dedication she put into it. Her opening chapter offered a powerful analysis of the challenges that all of the Lebanese immigrants faced coming to the South in 1890s and early 1900s. [46, p15]

As I conducted my research, Ms. Whitaker's findings on the early life of the Lebanese immigrants to Greenville turned out to be quite similar to that of the Raad/Josephs in Georgetown. Each family faced discrimination because, according to Whitaker, they were not native born, had dark skin and were not Protestants. She offers a wonderful historical backdrop:

> *The Lebanese quickly became known for being peddlers. Both men and women worked as peddlers. Peddlers required little capital, no skills and a minimal command of English. Not only was peddling a low-cost means of achieving the cultural ideal of entrepreneurship, it also offered opportunities for becoming fluent in English ... (those) who stayed in this country usually saved up their money and opened small stores or eating places that were patronized by office workers and business people.* [46, p8]

This was the same experience of many of the Lebanese immigrants to Georgetown, South Carolina. Her work was instructive on so many points and her research was thorough. Although most of her work was about the Lebanese in the upstate area of South Carolina, mostly Greenville, many of her conclusions and findings were spot on regarding the Lebanese of Georgetown, S.C., which my work addresses. It was especially important in light of the fact that she noted in her opening: "There is almost no published academic material on Lebanese Christians in the South." [46]

An observation made in Ms. Whitaker's introduction is worth repeating since it applies to me as well, since I am not Lebanese, but Irish Catholic, and have heard many of my family elders speak of the trials and tribulations of the early Irish Catholic immigrants throughout the country. Ms. Whitaker wrote:

I do not have any 19th or 20th century Middle Eastern ancestry, but I have spent much of my life contending with many of the obstacles faced by these immigrants and their children, especially since the Easter 25 years ago I was received into the Roman Catholic Church. I therefore understand and respect the experience of the Lebanese who came to South Carolina. [46]

As of this writing in 2017, many Middle Eastern people continue to suffer prejudice on the basis of their religion, race, color of their skin or country of origin. If this work can help shed light on how wonderful one small group of Lebanese families were and the challenges they faced, it will have been worth the hours of this labor of love.

PROLOGUE

In 2013, I set out to capture the history of a family that seemed so vast in my mind's eye as to defy the task. As I closed the research out in 2017, the story seems so simple.

Families in the Middle East in the 1890s, much like so many families in the South in the 1860s, were being torn apart. In both cases civil war had led to poverty, food shortages, loss of property and death of loved ones.

In the case of the Lebanese families in the Middle East, the decision was to seek a new life in a new land, America. By the 1890s the United States had abolished slavery and had tried its hand at reconstruction throughout the Confederate States. From hindsight, the decision to come to America seemed so simple – just go. But, in reality the decision was momentous, painful and challenging. Hopefully, this work will capture some of those challenges and share the wondrous path of these interesting families.

In 2016, I gave an hour-long presentation at the Georgetown Library and then gave the same lecture to a Coastal Carolina University Lifelong Learning (OLLI) class overviewing the history of the Lebanese Community in South Carolina's third oldest city. These were enjoyable exercises, with interested audiences. Those presentations have now led to a Georgetown Public Library "Lebanese of Georgetown Project," supported by a S.C. Humanities Council grant. In addition, we are working with NC State and their very scholarly project on the Lebanese Diaspora in the South. The plan is to offer a major presentation, publish a study and generate a documentary which includes video interviews with multiple second and third generation family descendants.

Over the past four years my wife and I have conducted dozens of interviews with a number of the 80- and 90-year-old family members and their children. We have traveled the state to family churches, weddings, funerals in search of information. This was coupled with many hours of interesting reading at various libraries and of course finding wonderful studies online. What became clear early on was that I was getting a front row seat to a family epic. As I interviewed the elders their passion and pride in their family was truly inspiring. I hope this work will shine a light on this classic American success story.

John Kenny

SECTION 1

INTRODUCTION AND HISTORY

Joseph Thomas Raad Family Tree
(Original painting in Camden, S.C.)

WHO ARE THE LEBANESE?

In 1987, John G. Moses, published a well-researched history entitled *The Lebanese in America* and dedicated it to his immigrant parents, Gabriel John Moses and Najia Chamoun Moses who had immigrated *"seeking to escape the economic stagnation and poverty in their homeland of Mount Lebanon, sought a better life in the New World, and despite initial insurmountable obstacles, ultimately realized their hopes and dreams in the free, fertile soil of America."* [36] The opening offers a concise overview of the rich 7,000-year history of the Lebanese people:

To understand the Lebanese in America, it is necessary to go back in time and distance to their country of origin, their ancestral land of Lebanon, and to examine its complex historical past with its continuous commingling of diverse peoples, races and religious sects on its ancient soil.

The small, strife-torn nation of Lebanon, located at the farthest eastern end of the Mediterranean and at the crossroads of three continents – Asia, Africa and Europe – was the ancient home of Lebanese Americans.

Successive waves of nomadic invaders from the Arabian Desert, sea peoples from the Mediterranean and mountain tribes from Iran and Anatolia have, in the course of more than 7,000 years of history, repeatedly assaulted Lebanon and given its inhabitants a diverse racial makeup.

If we examine closely the mélange of races that intruded upon Lebanon, mingled with the original inhabitants and left some vestiges of their culture on present-day Lebanese, we discern two dominant ethnic strands – the Semitic, represented by peoples largely of desert origin such as the Canaanites, Babylonians, Aramaeans, Phoenicians and Arabs, and the Indo-European element for the most part, peoples of mountain origin represented by the Hittites, Persians, Greeks, Romans, Byzantines, Franks and Armenians.

Despite the great diversity and numbers of races who have invaded Lebanon and inundated the country with their different cultures, the Lebanese have proven themselves throughout their long history as a people very adaptable to change. Whatever the circumstances – catastrophic or fortunate – in which the natives of Lebanon have found themselves in their long past, they have always adapted to changed conditions and managed to survive and thrive. [36]

PHOENICIANS, LEBANESE, AMERICANS
A Brief History

In 1961 John Fitzgerald Kennedy took his oath of office and became the first Catholic and Irish American to become President of the United States. In his Inaugural Address, much of the English-speaking world got to know his now-famous exhortation: "Ask not what your country can do for you; ask what you can do for your country." That quote was originally penned in the early 1900s by the famous Lebanese poet and artist Khalil Gibran (1883–1931). Few had heard the quote prior to this Inaugural despite the fact that Gibran's *The Prophet* is the best-selling volume of all time, after the Bible. That exhortation in Gibran's "Letter to Syrian Youth" remains the most-quoted sentence of any inaugural address in American history. It is a fitting way to start this history of how fewer than a dozen families left Lebanon and heeded their famous poet's quote a generation before the world heard of John Kennedy.

This story is about four Lebanese brothers and their wives, who came and stayed in America and heeded the quote of their famous author. They uprooted their lives in a tumultuous part of the world to leave behind suffering and killing and religious persecution to come to a country that offered opportunity and religious freedom. Many left behind siblings and parents. They came to Georgetown, South Carolina, and in many senses never looked back.

Historic Backdrop

Lebanon's flag was designed to be a neutral flag, not allied to any one of Lebanon's religious groups. The red stripes symbolize the pure bloodshed in the aim of liberation. The white stripe symbolizes peace and the white snow covering Lebanon's mountains. The green Lebanon cedar symbolizes immortality and steadiness.

A Very Special Family

Lebanon sits on the eastern side of the Mediterranean Sea which connects to the Atlantic Ocean. The Mediterranean almost completely surrounded by land – on the north by Europe and Turkey; on the south by North Africa, and on the east by the Middle Eastern countries. *It was an important route for merchants and travelers of ancient times that allowed for trade and cultural exchange among emergent peoples of the region. The history of the Mediterranean region is crucial to understanding the origins and development of many modern societies.* [4] Being the "Crossroads of the Mediterranean Basin," Lebanon has always had a rich history of religious and ethnic diversity.

The Lebanese are a proud race with a civilization dating back more than seven thousand years, predating recorded history. The Lebanese trace their ancestry to that of the legendary Phoenicians whose powerful maritime empire flourished for more than a thousand years (c.1550-539 BC) and spread its culture throughout the entire Mediterranean basin. Only the Roman Empire would eclipse its power in the region. It was the rise of that Roman Empire and the spread of Christianity throughout the Mediterranean that would be the next great influence in the lives of the Lebanese. With the birth of Christ and the expansion of the empire, a two-century long clash between Christians and Muslims began and would forever impact Lebanon and the Middle East.

In 64 BC, the region came under the rule of the Roman Empire, and eventually became one of the Empire's leading centers of Christianity. In the Mount Lebanon range, a monastic tradition known as the Maronite Church was established. As the Arab Muslims conquered the region, the Maronites held onto their religion and identity. However, a new religious group, the Druze, established themselves in Mount Lebanon as well, a religious divide that would last for centuries. During the Crusades, the Maronites re-established contact with the Roman Catholic Church and asserted their communion with Rome. The ties they established with the Latins have influenced the region into the modern era. [6]

After the fall of the Roman Empire and for a period of 400 years (the 1500s through the middle of the 1800s), the tiny area of Lebanon was part of the vast Ottoman Empire, ruled from the capital of Constantinople/Istanbul.

During the 16th and 17th centuries, in particular at the height of its power under the reign of Suleiman the Magnificent, the Ottoman Empire was one of the most powerful states in the world – a multinational, multilingual empire that stretched from the southern borders of the Holy Roman Empire on the outskirts of Vienna, Royal Hungary (modern Slovakia) and the Polish-Lithuanian Commonwealth in the north to Yemen and Eritrea in the south; from Algeria in the west to Azerbaijan in the east; controlling much of southeast Europe, Western Asia and North Africa. At the beginning of the 17th century the empire contained 32 provinces and numerous vassal states, some of which were later absorbed into the empire, while others were granted various types of autonomy during the course of centuries. With Constantinople as its capital and vast control of lands around the Mediterranean basin, the empire was at the center of interactions between the Eastern and Western worlds for more than six centuries. [6]

With stability, Lebanon became the academic and cultural center of the Ottoman world.

Modern History of Lebanon

As the power of the Ottoman Empire began to fade in the early 1800s, the enmity between the Muslim Arabs and Druze and the Maronite Catholics in Lebanon took a brutal turn. In the 1860s, at about the time of the U.S. Civil War, Lebanon had its own "civil war" resulting in villages being pillaged and ransacked and thousands being killed and wounded.

The 1860 Druze-Maronite conflict was the culmination of a peasant uprising, which began in the north of Mount Lebanon as a rebellion of Maronite peasants against their Druze overlords and culminated in a massacre in Damascus. It soon spread to the south of the country where the rebellion changed its character, with Druze turning against the Maronite Christians. Around 20,000 Christians were killed by the Druzes and 380 Christian villages and 560 churches destroyed. The Druzes and Muslims also suffered heavy losses. [7]

It was with this backdrop of a Lebanon in turmoil that Lebanese Catholics began a mass migration that would culminate in a diaspora of 3.3 million Americans of Lebanese ancestry. Lebanon would eventually lose one quarter of its total population to emigration. *Christian Lebanese were the first Arabic-speaking people to come to the Americas in large numbers. Their earliest immigration to the United States began in the late 1870s, peaked in 1914. A second wave of immigration began in the 1960s.* [7]

Though there is evidence of earlier migration from the Middle East to North America, the first documented cases of immigration from Lebanon to the U.S. occurred in the 1870s. As reported in The New York

> *Times, a physician who had been employed by the American Protestant College in Beirut received official permission to travel with his family to Alexandria in Egypt, and from there, the family made their way to Liverpool and then New York. Large-scale emigration from Lebanon to the U.S. began a few years later, in 1885, and continued until 1924 and the passage of the National Origins Act.* [46, p16-17]

In understanding how they came to the various sections of the United States, history shows that many were inspired by reports of religious freedom and an open culture and economy. A major role in this elucidation was played by American doctors and teachers who went to Lebanon as missionaries. Another great attractor turned out to be the "world fairs" that were in vogue and took place in Philadelphia (1876), Atlanta (1881), New York (1883), New Orleans (1884), Chicago (1893), and St. Louis (1904), exposing participating Mediterranean people to Americans and American society. These fairs highlighted the economic opportunities and the need for new workers that would come from the immigrants from Europe and Asia and the Middle East.

As we delve into the emigration to Georgetown, South Carolina, the role of an aggressive Mayor, son of an immigrant who showcased his city at various "world fairs," including Atlanta, was instrumental. He and his fellow Georgetown businessmen understood that the South, after Reconstruction, needed to attract new businesses, new merchants and build a new economy. It was their belief that a major factor in such a resurgence would be an immigrant merchant class and labor pool. Often a single family from a village would be exposed to the opportunities available to them in the United States and the family emigration would begin. They would send a son or two, and word of the opportunity would spread.

Many of the immigrants from various nations who responded to the avalanche of Southern states' marketing campaigns left their original destinations in the South as soon as they could, due to lack of opportunity, hostility from the locals, or being unaccustomed to living in a rural area. There was a national trend of growing hostility to immigrants and Catholics from about 1890 onward, partly caused by the hard times in the national economy and partly by alarm at the seemingly unceasing incoming tide of immigrants who were increasingly dark and non-Protestant. Many native-born Americans, who were accustomed to living in a solely Protestant environment and to hearing only English spoken, felt threatened by the newcomers.

The most interesting question, posed by Catherine Whitaker in her thesis on the Greenville Lebanese immigrants, is valid in Georgetown as well: *How did the Lebanese get from the margins of South Carolina life to its center?* [46]

Emigration to Georgetown, South Carolina

The brutal civil war in Lebanon between the Druze and the Christians and lack of opportunity and religious freedom resulted in about a dozen families emigrating over a 20-year period from 1890 to 1910 to the small seaport of Georgetown, South Carolina. Some would return to Lebanon, but almost all remained and called America their home.

> *When we come to the listing of the pioneers by name, it seems the first family to come to Georgetown were the Adrys. They must have come about 1895... Joseph Kozma, and his sister, Mary, came to the town about 1898. The Kozmas opened a store. On the rear of the same property is a small house and it became the hospitality spot for all incoming Lebanese... Some word of good opportunities at Georgetown was voiced about in Lebaa and the adventuresome followed the pioneers.* [28]

Many were true to their old ancestry as Phoenician travelers and merchants. In Georgetown that merchant culture would serve them well both from an economic survival standpoint and also as an entry ticket into the established society of this, the third oldest town in the State of South Carolina.

A Very Special Family

Life in Georgetown, SC, as the Lebanese Arrived

From the history page of the City of Georgetown website:

> *The Civil War changed the whole way of life for this region. The reconstruction period that followed was a social, political and economic upheaval. The rice crops following the war were failures, and rice could no longer support the economy of Georgetown. The combination of the disruption of the work patterns, competition from Southwestern rice growers, and several devastating hurricanes spelled the end of the once fabulous rice culture by the dawn of the twentieth century.* [2]

By all accounts, Georgetown suffered terribly during the post-Civil War Reconstruction period from 1865 to 1876. Prior to the War, the economy was based entirely on agriculture. Early on it was indigo, and by the 1800s it was rice. As a direct result of disastrous Atlantic hurricanes and the loss of slave labor, the rice crop essentially failed between 1866 and 1888. Many of the freed slaves moved out of South Carolina and those that remained often did not want their families working white men's farms. Instead, they turned to subsistence farming on small parcels of land that they owned or worked as tenant farmers. Rice continued to be grown commercially until about 1910, but never on the scale or with the profits attained before 1860. By the time the Reconstruction era ended, the Georgetown economy was shifting to harvesting and processing wood products; by 1900 there were several lumber mills in operation on the Sampit River. The largest was the Atlantic Coast Lumber Company

Photo courtesy of Georgetown County Digital Library

which provided a much-needed boost to the local economy. In 2012, historian Mac McAlister noted that it was around 1905, *Georgetown reached its peak as a lumber port."* [35, p8]

George C. Rogers, Jr. is a leading authority on South Carolina and Georgetown history. In 1970, he published a definitive work, *The History of Georgetown County, South Carolina*.

> *By 1876 it was clear unless a new source of wealth was discovered, the white population would disappear. Fortunately, there was some turning to new avenues of business. Some men like David Risley turned to pine forests, as lumbering became important again... A few men built up small capital resources in the town and thus laid the foundations for a new white economy. Merchants supplied the plantations with necessities and secured first liens on crops. Heiman Kaminski and Joseph Samson & Company were both accumulating funds while the planters decayed. In the 1880s such capital would spark an economic revival.* [40, p456]

Photo courtesy of Georgetown County Digital Library

A major shift from agriculture to harvesting and processing wood products began at the end of the Reconstruction era. South Carolina was blessed with abundant forests, and Georgetown had four rivers forming the 12-mile-long Winyah Bay as a shipping lane to the Atlantic and the world. Young Mayor Morgan, businessman, banker and unabashed promoter sought to capitalize on those assets, and he and the other Georgetown businessmen helped to attract several lumber mills. The largest was the Atlantic Coast Lumber Company. This new industry along with newly constructed rail lines, highways and telecommunications would provide a much-needed boost to the local economy. As the twentieth century dawned, Georgetown under the leadership of Mayor Morgan began to modernize.

It was during this period that the Lebanese arrived and began to set up their businesses on Front Street. The city added electricity, telephone service, sewer facilities, rail connections, some paved streets and sidewalks, new banks, a thriving port, and a new public school. Morgan even sought and obtained help from the U.S. Federal government in Washington and a combination Post Office and Customs House was built. Morgan's papers are housed at the University of South Carolina Library in Columbia and show that he worked tirelessly to try to win federal appropriations for creating a deeper channel through the Winyah Bay bar and for improvements to Georgetown Harbor. He was also insistent on improving other modes of transportation, especially the railroad. He was a promoter of Georgetown and the Western Railroad. He wrote to congressmen, organized petition campaigns, and even traveled to Washington to gain support for his improvements. [29]

Photo courtesy of Georgetown County Digital Library

History of Georgetown from the 2010 Historic District Survey:

> *While the cultivation of rice faded from the forefront of Georgetown's economy, the national building boom of the last half of the nineteenth century ensured that lumber and shingles made up the majority of goods exported from Georgetown. Georgetown's harbor, supplemented by rail service beginning in 1883, shipped enormous quantities of lumber. Unlike rice, raw timber was not shipped to Charleston for processing and export, so this new economy, which lasted until after the turn of the twentieth century, brought independent prosperity. Many of the substantial dwellings and commercial buildings within the Georgetown Historic District date from this period.* [25]

A similar example of how this emigration occurred in other parts of the United States is the Lebanese emigration to Pennsylvania:

> *Around 1900, a group of about a dozen Lebanese, having grown dissatisfied with the dismal prospect of earning a livelihood from the stubborn northern Lebanese soil, set out to stake their claim on the mythical riches in the new land of Australia. But, while waiting for days in the crowded, damp room that was used to hold passengers in transit, the Lebanese noticed that European passengers were boarding certain ships without any problems whatsoever. Puzzled, fortunately they found a Lebanese shipping agent in Marseilles and asked why it was that others wishing to board for Australia were able to do so with such ease, while they had been kept waiting for days. The group was told that those in the fast-moving lines were not headed for Australia, but for another land, America, which none of the group knew much about. Some of the group, bored with waiting for the Australian ship and growing ever more restless, suggested that they board the next ship going to America. A dispute then arose among the group – half decided to go to America, and the other half grew so disgusted with their situation that they decided to return to their village – Kfarsghab, Lebanon.* [5]

Similarly, in Greenville, South Carolina:

> *Greenville was a prosperous, growing Southern town in the midst of a booming industrial area. The Lebanese immigrants who arrived in Greenville, originally to peddle and, later, to buy and run stores and eating places, found themselves in what would have been a culturally congenial environment if it were not for the growing nativism and increasing anti-Catholicism. Not only did the Lebanese physically differ from most of their native-born white neighbors and customers, they spoke English with an unfamiliar accent and most of them worshipped differently than their neighbors.* [46]

The Lebanese Emigration

The first surge of Lebanese emigration to the Americas began following the settlement of what could be referred to as the first Lebanese Civil War. It was purely accidental that it was nearly identical in time span with the U.S. Civil War. This civil war began when simmering discontent in the Mount Lebanon area erupted into violence. Emigration began following the settlement of this conflict in 1865, in response to growing economic and social instability.

As a group, the Christian immigrants who arrived in the U.S. from the Middle East before 1950 were insignificant in numbers in most areas of the U.S., compared to larger immigrant groups. This was also true in South Carolina. However, in South Carolina, they have had an impact on their communities far out of proportion to their numbers. The Sheheens, a family of Lebanese descent, have become a political dynasty in Kershaw county; the Saleebys, one of whom was a long-time state legislator from Darlington county, have become seemingly ubiquitous in public life in the Pee Dee; the Barkoots in Columbia are well known in certain areas of real estate, and the Baroodys of Florence have contributed several medical professionals to the Florence area. These are just a few examples of the Lebanese families who have remained and have contributed to South Carolina's public life. [46]

There were two ways for immigrants to gain acceptance into local white society in South Carolina between 1880 and 1940. One of these ways was to join a socially acceptable church. Another way was to own a business. In the case of the Lebanese who came to Georgetown, they chose the latter. They kept their socially "unacceptable" religion of Catholicism and chose to excel as merchants, as their Phoenician forebears had done.

A wonderful overview of the businesses that the Lebanese built and ran was provided in the Whitaker thesis:

The Lebanese and their descendants who settled in South Carolina before 1950 founded and ran small businesses in the cities, towns and rural areas of the state. Almost all of these immigrants were Christian, and most were either Catholic or Orthodox. Most of their small businesses were stores and eating places, but a few were farms. The Lebanese quickly became known for being peddlers. Both men and women worked as peddlers. Peddling required little capital, no skills, and a minimal command of English. Not only was peddling a low-cost means of achieving the cultural ideal of entrepreneurship, it also offered opportunities for becoming fluent in English. A new immigrant, male or female, would enter upon some sort of contractual relationship with a merchant who would furnish him or her with a pack and some manufactured items to trade or sell. At first, these were religious items truly or allegedly from "the Holy Land." Later, the pack items would consist largely of small necessities for the busy farm wife, such as sewing supplies and ornamental lace. The early peddlers walked their routes, overnighting with farm families when they couldn't get back to their boarding houses. General stores run by native-born white men, especially in rural areas, were often unofficial men's clubs: they could be hostile environments for women. This especially helped Lebanese women peddlers as few other women worked as peddlers. Cash was in short supply, so a farm wife would frequently trade for her purchases with eggs and other produce. This type of trading is often thought to be a major reason for Lebanese going into food-related businesses. The peddlers who stayed in this country usually saved up their money and opened small stores or eating places that were patronized by office workers and business people. They usually settled in growing towns and cities. Before 1914, the Lebanese occupied a racial limbo in the United States. In most areas of daily life, they could function as white, but they were not guaranteed citizenship, no matter how long they lived in the U.S. or how badly they desired naturalization. [46, p8]

Similarly, 12 Lebanese families came to Georgetown, South Carolina at the turn of the century, stayed and prospered.

Photo courtesy of Georgetown County Digital Library

LEBANESE CHRISTIANS, MARONITES AND ROMAN CATHOLICS

"Our parents were strong and courageous people because they had Faith in God and the courage to persevere in the face of great obstacles. They did not see these obstacles as roadblocks; but challenges to be overcome. During the great Depression of 1930 they never lost Faith. They never lost sight of their goals. Their children have been testimony to this. Many have become doctors, nurses, dentists, and professional people. They have distinguished themselves and are respected in their communities. They have been a credit where ever they have lived. God bless them all." [27]

Faith in a god through organized religion is at the heart and soul of all humanity. For some faith is rejected, organized religion is spurned and life is lived day to day with no apparent reference to life beyond oneself. For the Lebanese, history never allowed that luxury. Their early Phoenician roots were as seafaring merchants considered to be the greatest traders of their time, some two thousand years before Jesus Christ was born. Initially, their religion was polytheistic, but as the Phoenicians spread all over the Mediterranean coastline, various branches, such as the Lebanese, abandoned their multi-god world in favor of Christianity, with some becoming Muslim, each embracing their history and culture as Mediterranean or Levantine. [38]

"Lebanon is mentioned more than 60 times in the Bible. The cedar of Lebanon is the symbol of steadfastness and strength, just as we speak of the "mighty oak." In St. Mark's Gospel (Mark 3-7) we are told that people from the neighborhood of Tyre and Sidon came down to Galilee to hear the prophet Jesus and on at least one occasion, He went himself into that area." [27]

The modern country of Lebanon became the most religiously diverse society in the Middle East, comprising 17 recognized religious sects, with the main two being Christianity and Islam. [38]

Ninety percent of the Lebanese who came to Georgetown at the beginning of the 20th century were Christians. At almost the same time as the United States War Between the States, Lebanon was engulfed in a brutal religious civil war pitting the Islamic Druze against the Maronite Christians. One estimate put forth by Sir Winston Churchill indicates that 11,000 Christian Lebanese were murdered, 100,000 became refugees, 20,000 were widowed and orphaned, 3,000 habitations were burnt to the ground and 4,000 more perished from destitution. [9] Other estimates put the estimate at 25,000 Christians killed. It was with the backdrop of this brutal sectarian and religious war, that the Josephs, Thomas, Khourys, Isaacs, Kozmas and other Lebanese began their search for a new home in the Americas. Their Christian faith, so tested over hundreds of years in the Middle East, became one of the foundations of their life in the New World, in their new home of Georgetown.

When they first came to Georgetown, there were many Christians and a strong minority Jewish population, but almost no Catholics. There was no Catholic church and no Jewish temple. At the turn of the century, as the Lebanese were arriving, the Prince George Winyah Episcopal Church was already almost two hundred years old, dating back to the earliest English immigrants to Georgetown. The most interesting aspect of my research into religion in Georgetown is the openness to religious diversity that existed at the turn of the century. I attribute this to the radical impact of the American Civil War on the entire south, especially those states like South Carolina that were at the heart of the Confederacy and secession from the Union. Religious and ethnic differences were quite irrelevant during the five brutal years of the Civil War and terrible ten-year Reconstruction period. During the war, Christians, Jews and atheists fought side by side for both the North and the South. During Reconstruction, all religions became important lifelines to cling to as the old society unraveled. The key battlegrounds during these twenty years was about northerners vs. southerners and about blacks and whites and race. Religious differences were subjugated in the trenches and battlefields where 620,000 soldiers died and the infrastructure of the entire South was devastated.

By the time the Lebanese were arriving in the South, the focus was on business, the industrial revolution and rebuilding the shattered economy, and not on religious differences. History shows that the Lebanese can trace their roots back to the greatest traders of the early Mediterranean world. Understanding trade would be a critical factor in the success of the Lebanese in their new home. Their dark skin, their strange customs, their Catholic religion was less important to Georgetown than their willingness to work hard and become part of the merchant and entrepreneurial class. At the turn of the century, Georgetown was rebuilding and retooling. It was moving from a culture based on rice and indigo and slavery and sailing ships, to one based on lumber and railroads and steamships, and most importantly on workers who made their living in shops and factories and not on the farm. Between 1890 and 1900, a dozen Lebanese families were welcomed to a town whose leading merchants were not of one faith or ethnicity, but rather a mix of Christians and Jews and a few Catholics.

Father Richard Madden, a Roman Catholic Priest of Irish heritage was a major player in Catholicism in South Carolina in the first quarter of the century. He penned the most thorough history of Georgetown and its Catholics. One view of the welcome that the new Catholics found in Georgetown was written in 1910 in a church bulletin:

Best of all, it had a broad-minded, liberal and progressive citizenship, who extend a most generous welcome to all good people who may come here from this or any other clime. Nearly all religious denominations have handsome churches, and a spirit of toleration and brotherly love exists which is found in few places. [3]

This may have been an overbroad and over optimistic view of the town. Father Madden offers the following: *Like all immigrants they were met with suspicion, and the Lebanese found their one true friend in the Catholic priest, and the one familiar action, the Mass. Their dark complexion added further to their ostracism at Georgetown, and at times, close to open persecution appeared.* [3, p5] Interestingly enough, Father Madden notes that another Catholic, William Doyle Morgan had become the most prominent citizen of Georgetown, its first Mayor and head of the Georgetown Bank. It was Morgan who became the ally to the new Catholic immigrants.

Within the first decade of the Lebanese arrival to Georgetown, the old Episcopal Church would find new neighbors in the new St. Mary's Catholic Church and the Temple Beth Elohim. These two houses of worship were built by many of the leading merchants and businessmen rebuilding Georgetown. William Doyle Morgan led the drive to build the first Catholic Church in town, opening its doors in 1902. Prior to construction of the church, Catholic masses for twenty years were held in the home of John and Mary Morgan, William's aunt and uncle. For a time in 1899 those masses were held in what was known as "Walker's Rink." At that time, the Catholic parish was called Chapel of St. Anne. On the site of the Rink, was William Morgan's residence, which was later purchased as the Rectory of St. Mary's. As of 1910, the 30 Lebanese families represented fully one-third of this parish of 100 members. In the early years of the Catholic Church in Georgetown, there were at least three African American Catholics.

The St. Mary's Church History offers a sense of the difficulty of building a church:

> *In today's world it is difficult to understand the hardships experienced by our founding fathers. The Morgan family and the vestrymen of the church pledged their personal obligation to borrow money to build the church... local parishioners... held bazaars, carnivals and raffles to raise $9,000 for the church."* [3]

The "carnival" referred to in the Church history was a stunning event. The *Georgetown Times* of December 5, 1900, was emblazoned with following headline: *ALL ABLAZE, AND THE LIGHT SHOWN O'ER FAIR WOMEN AND BRAVE MEN. The Carnival Opens Up Under Auspicious Circumstances – Success Already Assured – Beauty and Chivalry In Attendance.*

The wonderful part was the ecumenical nature of the event and the common show of support for building a church for one religious group:

> *The cordiality existing between the various denominations was fully demonstrated on this occasion, for in the festive hall one was greeted by people of every faith. Each and all were made welcome by the genial Father Wood, the popular head of the Church, the bright fair faces of lovely women greeted one on every side.* [3, p22]

Photo courtesy of Georgetown County Digital Library

A Very Special Family

By 1935, it was clear that the Lebanese Catholics were a major component of the parish. In a newsletter discussing graduation from the St. Mary's Religious Vacation School, among the 16 pupils honorably mentioned 12 were members of the Joseph, Isaac, Kozma families. Most of them were children of the four original Joseph brothers. By 1937, the Depression was over, and a major new employer opened in Georgetown: the International Paper Company mill. Bridges were constructed opening automobile traffic to the north on Highway 17. St. Mary's would grow to 350 resident Catholics. The new Catholic Church, named St. Mary, Our Lady of Ransom, would become the Lebanese focal point of religion, social life and education during the entire 20th century. The first couple to be married in that church were both Lebanese immigrants: Nicholas Joseph and Aneesie Nahra. Nicholas was one of the four Joseph brothers whose families became legendary in town. My wife's paternal grandfather was one of them, John Joseph.

St. Mary's was at the center of Lebanese life in town. The Catholics sought to organize their own private school, St. Mary's Parochial School. It was here that many of those serving mass today were educated in the

earliest days of the school. Now that I live in Georgetown, each trip around town with any of the Lebanese who were raised here, creates an opportunity to reminisce about the various buildings and homes in which they went to school, took a piano lesson or swam. The most notable of those was the home of William Doyle Morgan, Georgetown's first mayor. It was used as a school and as a home for the nuns who were the teachers. This stunning house sits a block from the Catholic Church that Morgan helped to build.

The snapshot doesn't begin to tell the rich story of the first fifty years. In the first half of the 20th century, the church was so much more than mass, weddings and funerals. A classic example of this is the men's social organization, the Knights of Columbus, today the world's largest Catholic fraternal service organization.

To place this in context, a brief history of "society clubs" in South Carolina is in order:

> *In early Charles Town persons of like national origin tended to organize their own clubs for purposes of charity and pleasure. There were clubs representing all principle national elements in the province. The Scotch had their St. Andrews Society, the English their St. George's Society, the French their South Carolina Society. As early as 1736 there was a Welch Club which celebrated the anniversary of their patron saint. There was an Irish Society in 1749 and a German Friendly Society in 1766.* [11]

In Georgetown, the preeminent social group was The Winyah Indigo Society founded in 1755 and still very active today. It is one of country's oldest societies and was originally founded by the local

A Very Special Family

planters of indigo. By 1947, the Catholics were well established in Georgetown and a men's society of their own was in order. At a restaurant owned by two of the Lebanese family members in town, Kelly and his brother Louis Khoury, the initial meeting of the Knights of Columbus was held with six members, including my wife's father Alfred Joseph and her uncle Paul Wakim. Within a year, it would grow to 54 members and continue to hold its meetings at the Khoury restaurant near the railroad crossing at Front Street. By 1960, they would build their own Council Home on Highmarket Street, just a block from the Catholic Church.

The stories of the Knights' "hall" and the family parties, weddings and shindigs resonate loudly for me. I was brought up in New York City and my father was a lifelong member of the Knights. Poker games, dances, and family gatherings were weekly affairs. The Georgetown Knights website history regales us with many of the stories:

- The annual Mardi Gras fundraiser to outfit the St. Mary's Championship Drum & Bugle Corps;
- Support for Tara Hall Home for Boys, started in Georgetown by an Irish Catholic Priest, and still proudly serving the community 43 years later;
- Support to the Sarah Haven Home for Girls, the Kidney Foundation and Association for Individuals with Mental Retardation.

For half a century, the Knights' Hall was the place for Knights and their families to meet and hold socials and for many to play cards and slots and share an adult beverage. The Knights sold the Hall in 2006, but the organization remains a strong arm of the Catholic Church in Georgetown. The Lebanese family members are still counted on for their roles, well represented by the next generation of Josephs, Isaacs, Khourys and even me, just an in-law among them.

It may help place the importance of the Catholic Church in the Lebanese life in Georgetown in a proper perspective by giving you a snapshot of a Sunday service in 2013, over a hundred years after the first families came to this port city. St. Mary's is a relatively small parish, with only a couple of hundred families on the rolls. There are three masses in the church each weekend. The Catholic Church in the 21st century relies heavily on the laity to support the pastor and to fill the various roles necessary to conduct mass. At one of those masses, I took an informal head count, and there was a representative of the Lebanese families in every one of the key laity roles of the mass: altar servers, lector, cantor, Eucharistic minister, and usher. The parish council has family members on it, the finance council is chaired by one, and the current Knights of Columbus counts dozens of its 100 members as part of the extended Lebanese family.

Lebanese and Irish Families of 1900 Become Model for Church Merger in 2017

In August of 2017, the newly appointed Pastor of the two Catholic Churches in the City of Georgetown shared with the congregation that the Bishop for the Diocese of Charleston had made a decision to merge St. Mary Our Lady of Ransom and St. Cyprian.

St. Cyprian Church had proudly served the West End of the City of Georgetown for more than 60 years. The West End had traditionally been the melting pot of the city, serving African Americans and then many of the new immigrants who arrived in the city from Ireland, Lebanon, Germany and most recently Mexico and South America. Rents were lower, houses could be purchased for less, and the church and community were welcoming. In the 1940s, '50s, and '60s discrimination still existed in the city and to some extent in the church. Many living in the West End were pleased to have their own church that catered to their cultural choices. Others came to the historic district and to St. Mary's. Over its many years, St. Cyprian offered special mission outreach to its unique community: It was immigrant Irish Pastor Owen O'Sullivan who took in a homeless boy living on the streets and in 1969 built Tara Hall Home for Boys, which proudly has served more than 600 boys from challenged homes. St. Cyprian is the home of Friendship Place which has been meeting the unmet needs in the County of feeding the hungry, sheltering the homeless, training the unemployed, and providing transportation to a free medical clinic for the poor and disadvantaged. St. Cyprian Catholic School was part of an evangelizing mission where nuns have provided all students an excellent opportunity to understand and grow individually, physically, socially, emotionally and morally in Christ, providing a clear set of moral guidelines and values that will enable our youth to meet the demands of the future.

As the Catholic population dwindled in the West End and as more parishioners chose to come to mass at St. Mary's, St. Cyprian's no longer had its own pastor and was served by the pastor at St. Mary's who would say a mass at 8 a.m. in St. Mary's and then a mass at St. Cyprian's at 9:15 a.m., back to St. Mary's at 11 a.m. and return to St. Cyprian's at 1 p.m. for a mass said in Spanish for a growing Hispanic community A daunting schedule for a single pastor.

When St. Mary's new pastor, Father Richard Wilson, in the summer of 2017 announced the Bishop's decision to merge the two parishes, it was with a heavy heart knowing how many had such strong feelings for the wonderful mission parish and its tradition of service to African Americans and immigrants. In addition, there is always an issue of assimilation when two parishes come together joining multiple cultures, races and traditions. It was here that he turned to the rich history of the Lebanese in Georgetown and the role played by the Irish. Irish immigrants had established St. Mary's in 1898 and opened its doors in 1902, just as the Lebanese immigrants were arriving in the City. It turned out to be a grand merger with the Irish and Lebanese building a vibrant parish.

On this Sunday in August, Father Wilson would proudly recount that, when the Lebanese arrived, they were very different from the Irish: they were dark skinned, spoke little English, dressed very uniquely, cooked different foods, and were part of the Maronite rite of the Catholic Church. Yet, they were welcomed as Catholics and became leaders in all aspects of St. Mary's Church and its community. Father Wilson went on to explain that today, as we merge with St. Cyprian's, we should look to that model and that tradition and welcome our neighbors from the West End, who once again are often darker skinned, often speak English as a second language, and of course have cherished traditions, foods and lifestyles that differ from many of the parishioners in St. Mary's.

The model, created almost 120 years ago by the Irish and the Lebanese, is still alive and well suited to today. Just as the very prolific Irish and Lebanese large families were the basis of the Catholic Church in Georgetown in the 20th century, most predict that Mexicans and South Americans with their large families will be the future of Catholics in Georgetown and the United States in the 21st century.

A TIMELY MEMOIR

At the time my wife and I were moving to her ancestral home in Georgetown, S.C., *New York Times* war correspondent Anthony Shadid published his wonderful "Memoir of Home, Family and a Lost Middle East," entitled *House of Stone*. The book deservedly became a national bestseller. The year before I began this work, Shadid died at age 43, while reporting inside Syria on the Free Syrian Army that was resisting the brutal government of President Bashar al-Assad. He had covered the war torn Middle East for nearly two decades. His insights into being both American and Lebanese are quite powerful.

The focus of his memoir was his purchase and loving rebuilding of his great grandparents' house in the Lebanese town of Marjayoun. Fortunately for my work on this book, the memoir is rich in its reflections on life in Lebanon over the last hundred years and on the challenges and triumphs of his ancestors, both those who remained in Lebanon and those who emigrated to America and Brazil. Many of his quotes from family members helped fill in gaps in the personal reflections from the Joseph family. Shadid had the advantage of a reporter's eye and the fact that he lived in his ancestral village for an extended period while he rebuilt his "House of Stone." Throughout the memoir, he shares with us powerful and poignant anecdotes that took place over the 100 years as Shadid family members came to terms with the ravages of war, the loss of property, the death of loved one and the attempts to build a new life in the new worlds where they had emigrated. Three observations by Shadid early in his memoir help to set the stage for understanding his thinking.

The first was his sharing of the Arab word, *atlal,* meaning the remnants of yesterday were never lost. [42, p124] This is central to his memoir. The second offers a deep perspective on what it is to be an American versus to be an Arab: *I was raised with an innocence at odds with the experience of my pragmatic Arab ancestors."* [42, p26] The third helps to explain why rebuilding his grandparents' house took on the significance that it did and how it is central to both his memoir and his journey to understand his family and what they went through. He explains the significance of a house, or home in the edification of the Arab word *bayt*: *In the Middle East, bayt is sacred. Empires fall. Nations topple. Borders may shift or be re-aligned. Old loyalties may dissolve or, without warning, be altered. Home, whether it be structure or familiar ground, is finally, the identity that does not fade.* [42, pxv]

As Shadid explains, the history of the Lebanese has never been simple.

For so long, Lebanon had wrestled with the rudimentary questions of identity: Whether its inhabitants were Arabs first or Lebanese above all, whether they belonged to east or west, whether they were bound to a destiny that stretched far beyond its borders – the Muslim world, for instance – or were part of the legacy as particular as the history of ancient Phoenicia." [42, p143]

Marjayoun is about 67 miles south of Lebaa (the ancestral home of the Josephs) and seems to have shared much of the same climate, culture and history. Both the Shadid family and those from Lebaa that I followed are Maronite Catholics, and each began their emigration for the same reasons and in the same timeframe: war, political upheaval, economic instability and the chance for a new life overseas. Unlike the Lebanese that I have followed to Georgetown, S.C., most of the Shadids settled in Kansas City, Kansas. We thus are provided with the parallel journeys across the Mediterranean and then the Atlantic for both the Shadids and the Raad/Josephs:

The America that drew my family was a journey of 7000 miles, and although mountain roads and voyages in steerage were treacherous, the hardest were those first miles away from home, away from faces that would no longer be familiar… So much had to be jettisoned for the sake of survival. Emotions were not acknowledged when so many others had suffered more. There was only survival for these travelers and faces to recall until the pictures they carried frayed or no longer held together.

In other words, it is not just the others who have been left behind; it is all of you that is known; Gone is the power or punishment of your family name, the hard-earned reputations of forbearers, no longer familiar to anyone, not in this new place. Gone also are those who understand how you became yourself. Gone are the reasons lurking in the past that might excuse your mistakes. Gone is everything beyond your name on the day of your arrival, and even that may ultimately be surrendered. [42]

In reflecting on the Josephs and the other Lebanese who came to Georgetown, I sensed in the conversations with the first America generation of Joseph children, that similar hardships were faced and similar emotional impacts were felt. Shadid's observation on the names was absolutely accurate. Booking agents, customs agents, and immigration officials both here and abroad neither cared nor understood the significance of the Middle Eastern names they were confronted with. Out of laziness or neglect, family names were mutilated, changed and lost. From hindsight, we are told that many of the immigrants were comfortable with the thought of starting life in a new country with a new name and a loss of the old identity had its merits.

The Shadid memoir is haunting in its reflections on the various horrible upheavals that the Lebanese have faced over the last 150 years. A great quote which gives a sense of what both the Shadids and the Joseph brothers left behind:

The war would be the end and the beginning. Even now the most elderly recall stories of those last breaths of the Empire – the seferberlik. It was the Ottoman name for the draft, but it came to mean something more: all the famine, terror, and disease that took lives and drained spirits in those years. Mere normalcy seemed disinclined to return. [42, p21]

Shadid's passages about his grandmother leaving her home as a 12-year-old are quite poignant:

"Whatever the father said to his daughter on the day of her departure, I will wager he said it not with words, but with that shiny ride, a message she might not have heard on a day of things fast and barely taken in. Such a surprise it must have been to learn that she had slept her last night in her parents' house. Such a shift in life on the morning that started out safe. Whatever it was that her mother said to her daughter, I would wager she said it with things stitched or embroidered, soft or warm, for a future she had no way to imagine. What mother could explain or acknowledge to herself that these things, so beautifully laundered and folded would likely be the last of her things to carry her touch? [42, p150]

GEORGETOWN: 1800s TO THE TURN OF THE CENTURY

Prior to the Civil War, economic and social life in Georgetown, S.C., revolved around the massive rice and indigo plantations. The majority population was African American slaves along with a minority of white slave owners. The Civil War, at a cost of 620,000 Americans killed in action, would change both the economy and the political and social structure. The basis of the pre-war economy was farming and mostly rice growing based upon slave labor. With the Emancipation Proclamation of 1863 and the end of the war in 1865, "all persons held as slaves within the rebellious states are and henceforward shall be free."

Rice cultivation and harvesting without the free labor provided by slaves turned out to be uneconomic. In addition, the South was plagued with a series of brutal hurricanes which devastated the rice fields. Thus, the wealth and power and social hold of the plantation owners ended. The U. S. Federal Government in the North imposed major economic, cultural and property change during the Reconstruction Era from 1865 to 1877. Rights were granted to the emancipated African Americans, who found themselves in the majority. Those who supported the Confederacy during the war were replaced in positions of government power. During Reconstruction, thousands of Northerners came to the South as missionaries, teachers, businessmen and politicians in an attempt to transform the South into a "fair labor" economy. These so-called "carpetbaggers" were resented and resisted by those who had been in control of both the wealth and power since Georgetown has been founded in 1729. The former slave population dispersed away from the plantations along the rivers and Bay into more rural areas of Georgetown or to the North.

With this upheaval and the population shifts, power moved from the plantations into the Port of Georgetown, which was twelve miles from the Atlantic Ocean and fed by four rivers from the northern portions of the state and North Carolina. Georgetown became the focal point of a new, burgeoning economy, based on timber, shipping and manufacturing. Such an economy required laborers and merchants. The society saw an influx of Jews, Irishman and soon, other immigrants from far-away lands. Georgetown became mixed racially and ethnically, thus changing the society that the English settlers had built and controlled since the early 1700s.

By the late 1890s the economy had been transformed from rice and agriculture to the harvesting and processing of wood products and the construction of several lumber mills on the Sampit River in the heart of Georgetown's Port. The largest lumber mill on the East Coast, Atlantic Coast Lumber Company, provided a much needed boost to the economy, creating new jobs and requiring merchant marine, rail and other support.

Modernization of Georgetown from the plantation economy to manufacturing and shipping and supplies was being driven by a new power base of politicians, bankers and merchants. From the end of the Civil War in 1865 to the turn of the new century, non-plantation owners, such as the Doyles, Kaminskis, Shackelfords and Morgans took control of the economy and the seats of government power. They brought manufacturing, electricity, telephone and sewer services and rail connections along with paved roads, sidewalks and schools. This was the Georgetown and the new life that the Raad/Josephs were migrating to.

Georgetown's Mayor at 1893 World's Fair in Chicago. A Marketing Mission

Mayor William Doyle Morgan was in awe as he stood on the banks of Lake Michigan. In front of him was an engineering marvel, rivaled only by the Eiffel Tower in Paris. What mesmerized him was a 264-foot-tall "Ferris" wheel, the first of its kind and the focal point of a World's Fair on the 600-acre fairgrounds in the City of Chicago. Formally it was called the World's Columbian Exposition in celebration of the 400th anniversary of the discovery of America by Christopher Columbus.

The year was 1893 and Morgan had been Mayor of South Carolina's second largest port town on the Atlantic Ocean, Georgetown, for the past two years. He came to the Fair in search of ideas, inspiration and people. It was just short of 25 years earlier that the brutal Civil War had come to an end, leaving his city devastated and in need of a new economy. The rice and indigo that had sustained Georgetown for 100 years was now just history. The end of slavery and brutal hurricanes put an end to their production and the trade with Europe that had flowed from it.

The Ferris Wheel was the main tourist attraction, but Morgan was there to gain access for Georgetown to the 50 foreign countries and 43 states that were represented at this Fair. It was

Photo courtesy of Georgetown County Digital Library

here that he would tell his story of the stunning little city sitting at the convergence of four rivers that flowed out to Columbus' Atlantic Ocean. He was there to encourage those countries to send their emigres and their ideas to the newly reconstructed South and specifically his city. Most of all he wanted those countries and states to send workers for the burgeoning industrial revolution that was just arriving in Georgetown. Morgan and the other new young leaders of Georgetown knew that rice and indigo were being replaced with lumber mills and shipping based on water and steam power and that he was at the door step of radical change in America's society and economy. Plantations would be replaced by cities and a new urban industrial state. But, in order for Georgetown to benefit from this revolution, it would need workers.

Morgan was captivated. It would turn out that he was one of 27 million people who attended the Fair over the six months of 1893. There, he was exposed to 50,000 exhibitors and carried the Georgetown message to the World. What he learned became the bedrock of the radical industrial changes he would bring back to his port city. Rail, telephone, electric lighting along with advances in the maritime industry would prove to be Georgetown's future. Morgan's papers reflect on what he learned while in Chicago but were silent on who he met. We do know that visitors from Lebanon were at the Fair.

A Very Special Family

From a separate source, we know that an Arabic-speaking Muslim, Said Jureidini, had traveled from Beirut to Chicago for the Fair and while there converted to Christianity and was baptized by the Third Baptist Church of St. Louis, Missouri. [8] Two years later Jureidini founded the first Baptist church in Lebanon. It is clear that many from the Middle East had traveled to the Fair. Some had country Pavilions, such as Egypt. What is also clear is that Mayor Morgan had gone to Chicago to encourage Europeans and Middle Easterners and all other immigrants to consider Georgetown as a wonderful place to live and work.

It would be just seven years after the Fair, that the first of the Raad/Joseph brothers would sail from Lebanon to America and make Georgetown their home.

CHALLENGES FACED BY LEBANESE WHO CAME TO AMERICA

Just about the time that the Raad/Joseph brothers were getting settled in South Carolina, the anti-immigrant, anti-Catholic, anti-dark-skinned movement was taking hold across the country. A classic example of this was a bill introduced into the U.S. House of Representatives in 1907 proposing to set up an English language literacy test (H.R. 9177). U.S. Representative John Burnett from Alabama introduced that bill after a trip to Asia and the Middle East with the statement: *God made only the Caucasian to rule this country; and I, for one, look with apprehension upon any effort to introduce… those thru whose veins flow the blood of any other than the Caucasian race.* [48, p36]

Zogby's research and comments are quite instructive:

"As aliens in a foreign land, the odds against their survival were formidable… And only those who recognized the courage and fortitude of these indomitable immigrants would have predicted the degree of achievement and prosperity their children and grandchildren would enjoy." [48, p17]

"… the sources of their pride in their heritage were the very factors alienating them from American society— the richness of the Arabic language that Americans could not speak or even pronounce, the Eastern liturgies of their churches that were so unlike American churches and the Arabic culture." [48, p18]

"White (Anglo-Saxon) southerners, were establishing racist policies and promulgating racist attitudes directed at the Lebanese and other Mediterranean and Eastern European settlers. From immigration policies which discourage certain immigrants from further settlement into Alabama, to name-calling and exclusion from restaurants and other public facilities, Birmingham's Lebanese Americans experienced bigotry and racism from their "white" neighbors… living in America meant having to defend and protect their civil and human rights." [48, p35]

"Anti-Catholic and anti "colored" feelings put the Lebanese, as shop owners catering to both blacks and whites, in an awkward position. Not only were they rejected by whites as the "yellow race" (they were even called "dagos" by some) but their faith also set them apart from the Blacks. The 1920s and 1930s saw the greatest degree of racism directed against the Lebanese. Although the program remained until after World War II. [48, p37]

The Centrality of Color in 1900 U.S. Immigration Law

If you are like me, and light skinned, Irish-American and burn easily in the summer sun, the issue of being "white" or a Caucasian is just something we have always taken for granted – a birthright. In fact, many of us grew up envious of the wonderful olive tones and perfect tanning skin of our many friends that we grew up with whose families came from around the Mediterranean – Italians, Greeks, and yes, my wife's family, the Lebanese. I often joked that Mary Lou's brother, Al, looked like the famous Egyptian actor Omar Sharif in his role in "Lawrence of Arabia." I meant it as a supreme compliment. It is easy to take something for granted if you never had to fight for it.

Skin color was a major barrier to acceptance in everyday life in the United States in 1900 and especially in the South where the Raad/Joseph brothers chose to live. Animosity between "white" European descendants and darker skinned people of any kind, was the accepted norm. Two centuries of enslavement of black Africans and red native American Indians had been at the heart of a Civil War that had led to more than 620,000 America deaths. The resulting victory by the North lead to the legal emancipation of those blacks, but not necessarily their acceptance in the white dominated society. Being perceived as other than "white" was a very damning conclusion. (*I discuss this in later chapters.*) In this section I want to explain the implication of not being considered white in legal terms.

The United States Immigration Law in the 1900s was largely based upon the 1790s Naturalization Act. This was the U.S. statute that codified U.S. Naturalization Law. It restricted citizenship to *any alien, being a free* **white** *person, who had been in the U.S. for two years*. This was interpreted to mean that slaves, indentured servants, most women, and non-"whites" could not become U.S. Citizens. After the Civil War and the Emancipation Proclamation, the U.S. Congress would modify this Act with the passage of the Page Law of 1875, the Asian Exclusion Act of 1882 and the Alien Contract Labor Law of 1885. This series of prohibitive laws was designed to restrict immigration from Asia based on race and the "whiteness" of people from that region of the world. The Lebanese posed a unique challenge to U.S. Immigration officials, since Lebanon sat at the crossroads of Europe, Asia and Africa. These laws posed a double threat to Lebanese both from an immigration standpoint and their ability to become U.S. citizens.

In 1914, George Dow, a Syrian (at that time, Syria and Lebanon were synonymous from a U.S. legal standpoint) living in Charleston, South Carolina, had his application for citizenship rejected based upon a conclusion that Syrians were not Caucasian, i.e., white. Following the court ruling in Ex Parte Dow, members of Charleston's Syrian community organized fundraising and awareness campaigns to raise support for a judicial appeal. Their argument that the contemporary understanding of anthropology and race posited that Syrians are members of a Semitic nation and are therefore entitled to inclusion as members of the Caucasian or white race. The Merriam-Webster dictionary defines a Semite as: *A member of any of a number of peoples of ancient southwestern Asia including the Akkadians, Phoenicians, Hebrews, and Arabs.* The people of Syria and Lebanon were descendants of the Phoenicians.

For a period stretching from 1878 until 1915, there was a series of U.S. Federal Court cases in which "whiteness" was adjudicated based upon both "scientific evidence" and "common knowledge" rationales. The later relied upon popular, widely held conceptions of whether a person's race entitled them to be treated as "white." Eventually, these cases and rulings made their way through a series of U.S. District Courts in South Carolina and to the Circuit Court of Appeals for the Fourth Circuit in the case of Dow v. United States in 1915. The final ruling reads: *At the date of the new acts and amendments… it seems to be true beyond question that the generally perceived opinion was that the inhabitants of a portion of Asia, including Syria [and Lebanon], were to be classed as* **white** *persons.*

Thus, after a tumultuous period of about 30 years, the very years that the Raad/Josephs and other Lebanese were emigrating to the United States, the Federal Court would rule, in a South Carolina case that yes, Lebanese are in fact, as well as under U.S. law, "white."

The scholar Dr. Talcott Williams in a 1930 article noted the historical importance of the region of Syria and Lebanon from which so many early immigrants came, and celebrated the cosmopolitan nature that its culture brought America. *Syria and Syrians constitute the first land and first people in Southwestern Asia who have entered into modern civilization. They stand alone in this. If Syria were an islanded-land, instead of being four thousand years a thoroughfare of conquering peoples, swept by many tides, it would be, in its place as striking an example of progress as Japan.* [47, p125]

In the 1951 issue of *The Syrian World* an unknown author heralded "unhonored and unsung" pioneers – the first generation of immigrants,"

"When we think of pioneers, we associate them with those rugged souls who helped build our country. But there is another pioneer to whom we Syrian-Americans have let pass "unhonored and unsung." His name is not shouted from the hilltops nor praised in books. Unconsciously, we have relegated him to oblivion. He is not a master of our rich civilization, nor a certain individual that contributed to the enrichment of our lives He lives with us today in America. Our fathers! They came here unaccustomed to the tempo of the new life; the merits or demerits of their heritage were buried in the quicksands of a different land. They started life over again; they dwelt in privation of the necessities of life; by bundled knapsacks they started businesses that we, their children, might enjoy a right to the comfortable life." [14, p122]

An interesting twist on being a minority in America came in a September 1917 feature story in the *Utica Saturday Globe* entitled: "Who's Who in Utica, Where the Blue-Eyed Saxon is Finding Himself in the Minority, The Syrian-Lebanese in America" by Dr. Philip Kayal.

"Think not, oh blue-eyed Saxon, that you are altogether and irrevocably it. When your ancestors were dwelling in the fens, wearing the skins of beasts, killing wild animals with their huge clubs and dragging their not unwilling brides from their fathers' caves by their long fair tresses, the forebears of these strange people (Lebanese) who have come to us were wearing the silk of the Orient, were dwelling in houses and worshipping in temples whose architecture the world has not since excelled, producing literatures and philosophies and works of art that still are standards. Oh yes, these people have a heritage more ancient than yours." [30, p130]

Discrimination Among Immigrants

In the interviews I conducted with the Lebanese families in Georgetown, almost all of the first generation had nothing but fond remembrances of both their upbringing and of their interaction with the Catholic Church, school and social activities. The second generation indicated the same feelings. Therefore, it came as a surprise and a disappointment to learn from a number of the 80+ year-olds that, in the early days of St. Mary's Catholic Church, there was discrimination against the new Lebanese immigrants by the Irish Catholics who had first housed and nurtured the Catholic community in the late 1800s.

Two startling stories hale from the earliest days (1902, when the church was constructed, and in the next five years as the laity began to understand its role). The most blatant discrimination was where the new immigrants should sit. A large crucifix was set up in the center aisle of the church, approximately two-thirds of the way down from the altar. The new immigrants were told that they were to sit only behind the crucifix for Sunday Mass.

The second example came to light in a discussion with a long-time member of the church. She explained that, when the Altar Society was being formed, the Irish Catholic Mayor's sister stated that the Lebanese women could not join. This did not sit well with one of the prominent families, who were members of St. Mary's from its beginning. Mary LaFite Cathou, the wife of the owner of the very prosperous Fish House, who was of French ancestry, made it clear to the Irish, that the Lebanese and all were welcome both in the church and in the Altar Society. For emphasis, she made it clear that there would be no Altar Society if Lebanese women were not allowed to join. She made a wise decision; as pictures taken over the years would show that it was the Lebanese women who became major assets and often the majority of those serving.

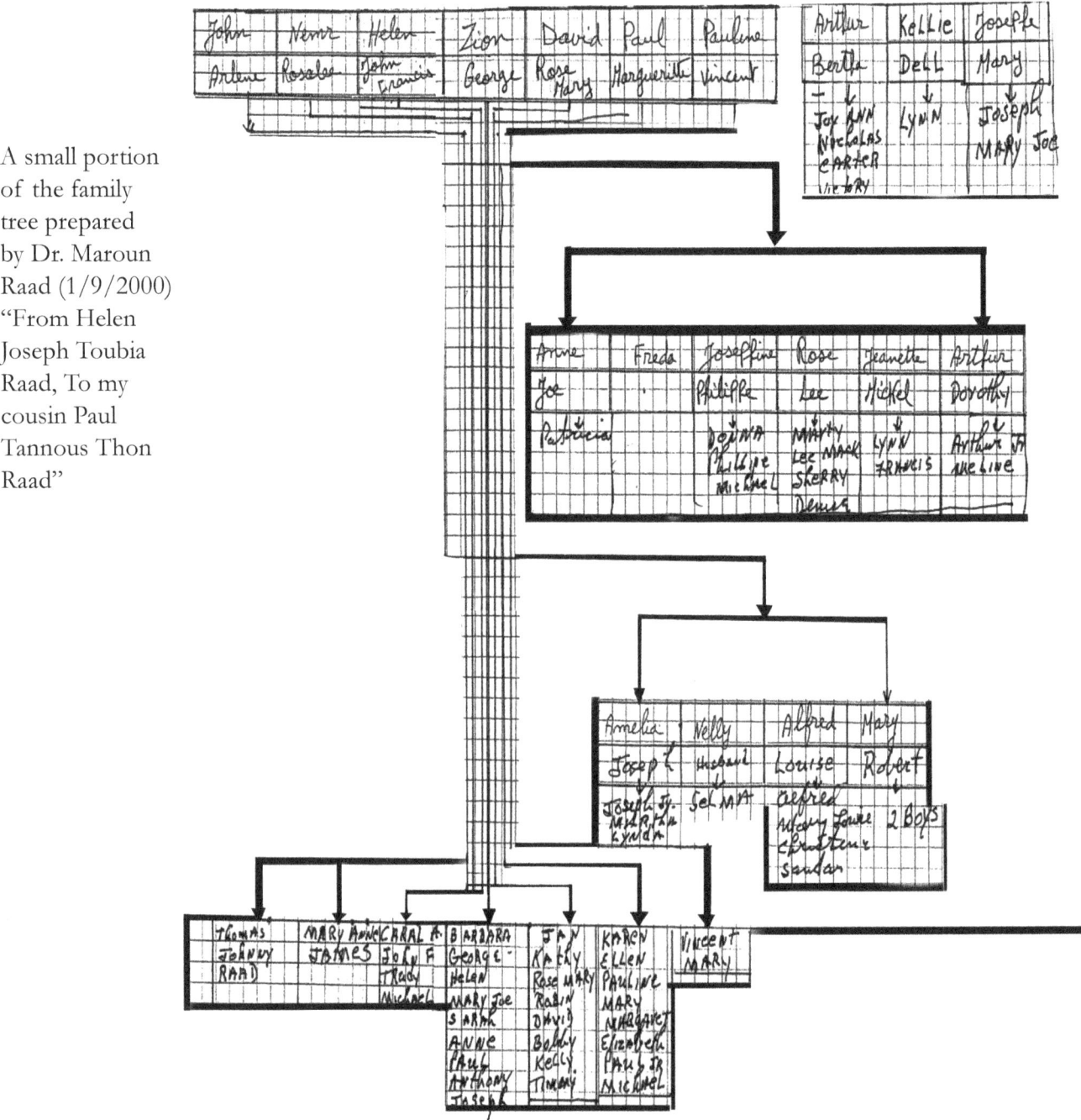

A small portion of the family tree prepared by Dr. Maroun Raad (1/9/2000) "From Helen Joseph Toubia Raad, To my cousin Paul Tannous Thon Raad"

SECTION 2

THE RAAD/JOSEPH FAMILY

At roughly the turn of the 20th century, four Lebanese brothers journeyed from their home outside of Beirut, Lebanon, and each eventually ended up in a wonderful seaport town where four rivers converge to form a beautiful bay that winds its way to the Atlantic Ocean. That town, now the City of Georgetown, South Carolina, sits at the headwaters of the Winyah Bay. The rivers are Waccamaw, Sampit, Black, and Pee Dee, and the brothers were Nicholas, Thomas, Shickory and John. They were the descendants of Joseph Thomas Raad (Youssef Tannous Raad), and each was referred to formally by his father's name, e.g., Nicholas, son of Joseph.

Nicholas Joseph Raad was married to Aneesie Nahra, Thomas Joseph Raad was married to Barbara Nahra, Shickory Joseph Raad married Sarah Frances, John Joseph Raad was married to Selma Azouri. The brothers had two sisters who remained in Lebanon. Shickory and John are half-brothers to Nicholas and Thomas. The four brothers remained married to the same Lebanese women, had 21 children among them, and 65 grandchildren. The Raad brothers were joined in Georgetown by other Lebanese immigrants from their small town of Lebaa and surrounding towns. Each of their journeys and paths were as memorable as those of the Josephs.

Over the next hundred years, these four men created a family dynasty epitomizing the best of American freedom, democracy and capitalism. In the post-civil War and post-Reconstruction period of Georgetown's history, these immigrants were an integral part of its resurgence as a major seaport and then a manufacturing town. At the heart of their success were family, church and county. From immigrant peddlers with their meager fortunes on their backs, these four men helped the city of Georgetown survive the economic turbulence of the Great Depression, helped build a Catholic Church community, and helped make Georgetown a wonderful place to live for their families and those who came to know them. Many of the first generation stayed put in Georgetown, and those who left often stayed in South Carolina. These Lebanese families left a permanent and positive mark on their city, their church and their community.

THE PARENTS AND THEIR PROUD 300-YEAR HERITAGE
Joseph Thomas Raad and Mary Habib

The Lebanese of Georgetown, especially the sons and daughters of the four Joseph brothers who came to America in and about 1900, were very proud of their heritage, their faith, their family and what they were building in their new country. In the first 50 years the way they celebrated and solidified the importance of their heritage was to gather early and often in their homes, businesses and in St. Mary's Catholic Church. Starting in the 1970s, knowing that many in the second and third generation had dispersed from Georgetown and had married non-Lebanese spouses (Irish, Germans, Italians and Greeks), the vehicle they used to pull the family back together was the family reunion. At those reunions oral history was shared, family connections were made, the diaspora got a chance to coalesce. It was from those oral histories and reunions that we learned about life in the old country and bits and pieces about the parents of the four brothers.

What we learned from those oral historians and shared family trees was that Joseph Thomas Raad, the son of Tannous Raad and grandson of Thon Raad, was married to Mary Habib. The family tree, prepared by Dr. Maroun Raad and Helen Joseph Toubia Raad, illustrates 150 years of Joseph history, but explains the Raad family dates back 300 years in the tiny village of Lebaa.

Joseph Raad had six children, four boys and two girls: Nicholas, Thomas, Shickory, John, Helena and Saada. In interviews conducted while preparing this book, I was told by various family members that Joseph had a second wife. It was unclear as to whether his first wife died. It appears that the two youngest brothers, Shickory and John did have a different mother. There is no hard information available on this. We do know that neither of the daughters ever came to America. Although Nicholas came to America when he was 27 years old, his brothers were much younger when they came in their late teens.

The reunions began in 1974 and have continued about every five years since that time. At the second reunion we learned a lot about the history of the little village of Lebaa from Nicholas' daughter, Victoria Inez Joseph. Miss Joseph was born in Georgetown on April 16, 1908, a daughter of the late Nicholas Raad Joseph (1873-1920) and Aneesie Nahra Joseph (1884-1959). Victoria became the Joseph family historian:

> *"By our descent we are Lebanese, our ancestors came to his country from Lebanon. The land we are talking about measures about 3700 square miles. South Carolina measures 3200 square miles. The population (in 1979) is about a million. That of South Carolina is about two million. But Lebanon is at the cross roads of the world. Three continents: Europe, Asia and Africa touch at this area, known as Asia Minor and as the Near East, it has been the battlefield for armies since history began. On a map made available by the Shell Oil Company in 1960, the road to Lebaa goes almost directly east from Saida. Lebaa is too small to be noted on the map..."* [29, p1]

Victoria's father, Nicholas Raad Joseph was born in 1873 in Lebaa and was the first of four brothers to come to Georgetown. Her mother, Aneesie Nahra Joseph was born in 1884 in Lebaa, a daughter of Thomas and Frances Khoury Nahra, and came to America in 1904. Victoria had three brothers, Arthur Joseph, Dr. Kellie Joseph and Joseph N. Joseph.

The first and second family reunions had been held at the Sea Gull Inn in Georgetown in the summers of 1974 and 1979. It was wonderful that Victoria did her research and made her presentation in 1979, since she died three years later at the age of 59. Her account clears up how the four Joseph brothers first came to Georgetown, when they arrived and who preceded them.

> *What kind of life did our people live before coming to America? They had farms and kept a few livestock. It is very unlikely that they knew anything about industry. They knew how to barter and haggle with traveling salesmen and that was helpful to those who came to America. They soon found themselves back packing items and going from door to door offering tapestries, attractive table cloths and napkins and shawls for sale. No doubt our families coming late, lost out on the big metropolitan areas and were sent into the Carolinas (Thank God).*

When we came to the listing of the pioneers by name, it seems the first family to come to Georgetown were the Adrys. They must have come about 1885. They operated a small knick knack store where the South Carolina Bank stands on the corner of Front and Orange St. Whether the Ardys did badly and got discouraged or did well and could afford to leave, they returned to Lebanon about 1898. Two sons had been born in Georgetown and some years later after the death of the parents, the boys came back to Georgetown. In order for them to do so it would seem they had to prove they were born in the United States. The Chief of Police, Robert Shurford, had Mary Kozma verify that she had stood as godmother for two boys at their baptism which had taken place in the Morgan home, the present rectory of St. Mary's Parish. Obviously this was before the church was built.

Joseph Kozma, and his sister Mary, came to the town about 1898. The Kozmas opened a store. On the rear of the same property was a small house and it became the hospitality spot for all incoming Lebanese. Periodically there were trips to New York to gather materials to be sold. The principle wholesaler that the Georgetown group dealt with was a Mr. Maoose. What could not be carried back to Georgetown was brought in by the Clyde Line steamers. Freight rates by ship were quite inexpensive. The steamers came directly to Georgetown.

Some word of good opportunities at Georgetown was voiced about in Lebaa and the adventuresome followed the pioneers.

The first of our family to come was the oldest son, Nicholas. He came about 1900. He seems to have joined the group at the Kozmas, which now included Joe Kozma's father-in-law, Assad Massad. Their first adventure was peddling. The men went, a few together, to a town where they rented space in a warehouse where they could leave their supply of commodities. They went out, going from door to door with their items in a back pack. When all the goods were sold they returned to Georgetown ready to stock up again and go back out on their rounds.

Nicholas must have done well. Within four years he was encouraging two brothers to join him. The brothers were Thomas and John. Perhaps Nicholas helped finance the trip. He did have a very great interest in their coming. They were to bring and did bring the young Aneesie Nahra with them. Nicholas and Aneesie became the first Catholic couple to be married in the new Catholic Church of St. Mary!

In due time Thomas was ready to return to the girl he had left behind him Barbara Nahra, a cousin to the aforementioned Aneesie. Thomas and Barbara were married in Lebaa and prepared to venture on to America. The returning party was considerably larger. Besides Thomas and Barbara, there was the fourth brother – the one at whose birth the parents called, "Thanks the Lord!" – Shickory. With Shickory was his wife Sarah Frances. Also in the party was the young Thomas Elias Isaac. In the meantime, John also got married. He had met Selma Azouri whose family was also recently come to America and living at that time in Kingstree. One might imagine that John and Shickory found Georgetown crowded with Josephs and both tried their fortunes elsewhere. John and Selma tried Columbia and were later joined by Shickory and Sarah; they operated a restaurant in Columbia. After about nine years in the venture John and Selma moved to Hopewell in Virginia and then to Hemingway, S.C. Eventually they returned to Georgetown and opened a small general store. A few years later Shickory, Sarah and their family also return to Georgetown to open a general store. Another such general store was opened by Paul and Helen Nahra, parents of Thomas Joseph's wife." [29, p1]

Victoria's narrative, found in the stack of family reunion papers in my wife's parents' home is faded and turning yellow 37 years later. Many had forgotten the history that she provided and often asked how and why the Joseph brothers came to Georgetown. With luck the document has survived, and we now know that the earliest Lebanese pioneers to come to Georgetown were the Adrys. Unfortunately, I could find nothing in writing about them.

The Adrys only stayed a couple of years in America and returned to Lebaa. The next pioneers were brother and sister Mary Kozma and Joseph Zayden Kozma. They came to Georgetown around 1898. It was the Kozmas, arriving two years earlier than Nicholas Joseph, who became firmly rooted in Georgetown and became the landing site and initial home for succeeding members of the immigrants from Lebaa, including the Josephs. Joseph Kozma and his wife operated the Kozma Grocery on Front Street in the same building where they and other members of the family called home for 67 years.

THE INITIAL JOURNEY AND ARRIVAL

I believe that even as your fathers come to the land to produce riches, you were born here to produce riches by intelligence and labor. Kahlil Gibran [23]

When the four young sons of Joseph Thomas Raad left their homes and families in Lebaa between 1895 and 1905 and settled in Georgetown, S.C., we know they came by ship, in steerage. There was regular steamship service in and around the Mediterranean Sea by the middle of the 19th century. Steamship agents promoted their service throughout the region and sold tickets for passage to new worlds. Often the voyage for Lebanese was from Beirut to the European ports of Marseille or Le Havre in France, then on to New York, Boston, New Orleans, Philadelphia, or to ports in South America or Mexico. Various of the families that arrived in Georgetown took slow circuitous routes. Some would live in South America or Mexico or Cuba for a time before their arrival in North America. The ships they traveled in were often dirty, overcrowded and unsafe, with meager food for the two- to three-week Atlantic Ocean passage.

The immigrants brought little in the way of possessions with them, but all had a view, long held in Lebanon, that working for someone other than themselves was not the best path to prosperity. In terms of income, there was a recognition that peddlers earned more dollars a day of work than did factory laborers. Statistics indicate that 80% of the first wave of Lebanese immigrants to America started out as peddlers. This path was especially open to them in the post-Civil War, post Reconstruction era in the South.

A Very Special Family

According to the 1860 U.S. Census there were 3.9 million slaves in America, representing about 13% of the total population. [16] Most lived in the South, with more than 400,000 in South Carolina. With emancipation and the abolition of slavery, new forms of trade and new markets had to be created. Over the thirty years from the end of the Civil War in 1865 to 1895, there was rapid growth in share cropping. The former slave owners on the plantations needed someone to work the land and tend their crops, but had little cash to pay. Sharecropping developed as a system where former slaves could negotiate a place to live and work and sometimes to purchase land. Much of these former slaves did not relocate to the North, but rather relocated from plantations to various rural areas of the South. This was obviously true in South Carolina, especially in and around the former plantations that dot the coast and the rivers running to it.

In a rural state where many residents remained distant from general stores, peddlers linked country dwellers to a world of manufactured goods that expanded greatly after the Civil War… They turned backyards and front rooms into merchandise showrooms and accepted payments in trade. These practices made them especially welcoming to rural women, whose trips to town or county stores often were rare. With little capital themselves, immigrant peddlers often catered to poor whites and blacks whose access to store credit was limited. Some peddlers managed to accumulate enough cash to start their own permanent stores. [37]

This appears to have been the path traveled by many of the Lebanese immigrants in the post-Civil War South and the earliest Lebanese immigrants to Georgetown, S.C. They came by circuitous routes, some through Ellis Island in New York, but others through Texas, Cuba and Mexico.

Their first experience must have been very disheartening, but they proved worthy descendants of their adventurous ancestors, the Phoenicians and Arabs. As peddlers, trying to sell crosses, rosaries and icons from the Holy Land and later laces and notions, they wandered from street to street and from town to town until they covered almost every city in the United States. Snow and rain did not stop them, nor did they lose heart. Signs at the doors reading 'No beggars, no peddlers' meant nothing to them, as they could not read English. It was the peddlers that laid the basis of our economic prosperity in the country. All honor to their memory! At the turn of the century, the Syrian [and Lebanese] peddler transformed into a petty shopkeeper… By the beginning of the 1st World War, a new step had been taken. The peddler had become a storekeeper and the storekeeper had become a manufacturer of kimonos, negligees, laces, dresses and other apparel. [26]

Research shows that many of these early Lebanese immigrants were especially drawn to set up businesses related to food and beverages. They were grocers and butchers and restauranteurs. A classic example was in Birmingham, Alabama where by 1925, Lebanese immigrants owned all, but two of the city's grocery stores.

A similar pattern was followed by the Raad/Josephs and other Lebanese families in Georgetown. As you will see in later chapters, first immigrant brother Nicholas Joseph set up a dry goods store, expanded it with his brother Thomas, the second brother to come, and then opened a grocery store and eventually rented space to a pair of Lebanese immigrants, Escie Thomas and Catherine Wakim Thomas, who set up Thomas Café. On Highmarket Street, a third brother, John Joseph opened a meat market and butcher shop.

It is clear that the early immigrants wanted to operate on their own terms both as peddlers and eventually shop owners. This was their path to acceptance in the New World and the stepping stones to economic success and entry into the middle class.

JOSEPH THOMAS RAAD'S
4 SONS AND THEIR WIVES, 21 CHILDREN
AND 65 GRANDCHILDREN

1873 NICHOLAS JOSEPH	1885 THOMAS JOSEPH	1888 SHICKORY JOSEPH	1890 JOHN JOSEPH
ANEESIE NAHRA	BARBARA NAHRA	SARAH FRANCES	SELMA AZOURI
Arthur 4 children	John 3 children	Ann 1 child	Amelia 3 children
Kellie 1 child	Nimmer 2 children	Freda	Nellie 1 child
Joseph 2 children	Helen 4 children	Josephine 3 children	Alfred 4 children
Victoria	Zion 9 children	Rose 4 children	Marie 2 children
	David 8 children	Jeanette 2 children	
	Paul 8 children	Arthur 2 children	
	Pauline 2 children		
7 Grandchildren	36 Grandchildren	12 Grandchildren	10 Grandchildren

COAT OF ARMS
Raads become Josephs

The Raad Coat of Arms evolved with the four quadrants representing the four brothers: the eagle, the thunderbolt, the lily and the outstretched hand with the Raad family motto: "Faith and Courage."

At the family reunion in 1979, Victoria Joseph shared with the assembled Josephs of three generations an explanation of the family shield, or coat of arms as it originally existed. I have been unable to find a picture or copy of the original coat, but the one featured on the cover proudly hangs on the wall in my wife's family home in Georgetown, S.C.

JOSEPH RAAD, The patriarch of the family, father of the four brothers, as explained by Victoria,
The shield's right side is intended to represent the family of Joseph Raad. We have the color blue because it makes a good show. On this field we have placed a streak of lightning – or a thunderbolt – for we understand in Arabic Raad means just that. Beneath the thunderbolt is a Lily – the symbol of St. Joseph. The left side of the shield is marked by symbols for each son and his wife.

NICHOLAS AND ANEESIE
The shield of Nicholas Joseph bears three gold balls. The time honored symbol of St. Nicholas. The gold balls represent three bags of money that St. Nicholas gave to three maidens who could find no suitors because they had no dowries. In time the three gold balls came to be the sign of a money lender – so, the pawn shop. In another direction the giving was extended so that St. Nicholas became Santa Claus! To show that we are not male chauvinists we put into the shield a symbol of the wife. We understand that Aneesie is a variation of Agnes – and since early Christian times, Agnes has been associated with its homonym Agnus, a lamb, we have added a lamb to this shield.

THOMAS AND BARBARA
On the shield of Thomas Joseph to the top of the left side we have placed two spears – symbols of St. Thomas the apostle who was martyred by a spear thrust. St. Barbara is the patroness of artillerymen. So the cannon signifies Barbara.

SHICKORY AND SARAH

Shickory is derived from shareen, "thanks." It is not uncommon to express "thank you" by a handclasp. So we use that. Sarah, we think is an easy one. Sarah can be a variation of aster – a star. We used the five-pointed star – the mullet.

JOHN AND SELMA

The apostle St. John is symbolized by the eagle, thus the eagle is at the top of the third shield. Selma is a variation of "peace" or "welcome." We hope the open hand expresses a sense of welcome.

Just one more feature. Almost all coats of arms carry a motto. We think that the history of the Lebanese is marked by faith and courage. [29]

A WELCOME MAT IS PLACED OUT TO IMMIGRANTS

An oft-asked question during my research was: "Why did the Raad/Josephs come specifically to Georgetown, S.C.?" Not having interviewed the immigrants themselves, it is not clear, but we do have some strong indications as to why.

During the late 1800s, the United States was in an expansion mode, undergoing an industrial revolution and a change from an agrarian economy to a manufacturing economy. This was especially true in the South, where the plantations had been devastated by the loss of slave labor and severe and recurring hurricanes. There was a recognition that the new economy needed new labor and the most likely source of the labor would be immigration.

Christian missionaries and teachers had been dispatched from the United States to Europe, the Middle East and Asia to spread the gospel and carried a message that America and its capitalist economy and its democratic form of government offered phenomenal freedom and opportunity to those willing to relocate and to work. They presented this young country as an open, prosperous and welcoming land, especially to immigrants fleeing religious persecution, war, poverty and often starvation. Waves of immigrants from Ireland, Europe and Asia heard the message and streamed into the country. That message also made its way to the Middle East and the small country of Lebanon and the tiny village of Lebaa. There, the Ottoman Empire was disintegrating and civil war between the Christians and the Muslim Druze was in full fury.

A second welcome was also extended by economic ambassadors of the various states and cities throughout America. This economic welcome mat was best evidenced by various "world expositions." A successful "first world expo" was held in The Crystal Palace in Hyde Park in London in 1851. It became the prototype for a series of international expositions that eventually morphed into "World Fairs." As the era of industrialization (1851-1938) took hold, the Fairs became focused on trade, technological inventions and advancements in science. They also provided much needed opportunities for social exchange among people of varying ethnic, religious and cultural heritages.

This was clearly true in Georgetown, S.C. Bankers, politicians, merchants, manufacturers recognized that the new post-Civil War economy would require a different labor force and new merchants to fulfill the needs of new forms of business. The leaders of Georgetown recognized the significance of these Fairs and William Doyle Morgan in the 1890s attended a number of the expositions that were held in Chicago, Norfolk, Washington, D.C., and New Orleans. Born in 1870 just after the Civil War and during Reconstruction, he was raised by a family of Irish immigrants who had moved from the North to Georgetown prior to the War. Working closely with other non-plantation owners such as the Kaminskis. Jews and Catholics and anyone else interested in the new economy were welcomed to the city. Morgan, who became Georgetown's first elected mayor had a simple message as he attended the fairs and expos: Georgetown is a growing, vibrant, modernizing port city and gateway to the Atlantic Ocean. It needed new blood to start and operate new businesses and the laborers to support its growth.

Nowhere in my conversation with the first generation Lebanese in Georgetown could I find the direct connection between the recruiting efforts of the missionaries or the economic ambassadors and their recruiting efforts. But it is clear their message had been received in the tiny village of Lebaa. Somehow, the Catholic missionaries that traversed the Middle East and would eventually form the first University in Beirut, Lebanon and the Irish American Mayor got the word out: "Georgetown is open for business and would welcome your arrival."

And so, the Lebanese came. Adrys, Kozmas, Raads, Josephs, Isaacs, Khourys, Asseys – each heard the message, first- or second-hand and each came. And interestingly enough, they stayed.

VIGNETTE: THE ONE-HUNDRED-YEAR TRIP

"A lot of amazing things happen with you, Raad family, especially with your women because you are strong and believers," Reverend in the village of Lebaa speaking of the family.

In 2009, the Raad/Joseph clan in America received a wonderful and unexpected gift. Their cousin, Helen Raad Bou-Karam, who lived all of her life in Lebanon, was coming to America for a family visit and to participate in a family reunion. Helen was the daughter of Joseph and Georgette Iserhalb and the granddaughter of Elizabeth Raad. She presented to her extended family her charming autobiographical piece, *The One-Hundred-Year Trip*. It is a glimpse into the minds and lives of family members who either never came to America or who came and returned to Lebanon, willingly or unwillingly due to decisions made by parents or based on family necessity. In 2017 my wife and I had a chance to meet and interview her. She is a delightful, energetic, smart woman with a head full of great memories and the entire family history. It was she, aided by a cousin, Dr. Maroun Raad, who prepared the stunning 50-inch 350-year family tree that was so helpful to me in preparing this book.

To ground this saga properly, one needs to trace the Raad family roots back over hundreds of years. Raad is an Arabic word that means "thunder." The Raad tribe came from Bami Hareth in Fahm. [39] The Raad family had always lived close to the sea. Over hundreds of years, Raads had lived in Tripoli, Beirut and Saida. According to Helen's grandmother, the branch of the Raad tree we are discussing came to Lebaa, Lebanon, a village in the Jezzine District some 350 years earlier. [18, p15] They had traveled from the North of Iraq fleeing Islamic massacres, arrived in Syria and eventually lived in the North of Lebanon in the village of Becharry where the famous Lebanese-American artist, poet and writer Kahlil Gibran came from. Prior to coming to America, that sea was the Mediterranean and it was about 15 miles from their tiny village of Lebaa. When they came to America they settled 12 miles from the Atlantic Ocean, in the then-small town of Georgetown, South Carolina. As explained in another chapter, the exact reasons for coming to Georgetown are not clearly known, but a number of theories have arisen.

Helen provides us with a wonderful first-hand account of what Lebaa was like in the 1890s of her youth by recounting a conversation that she remembers with her grandmother Elizabeth:

A Very Special Family

I was born in this lovely village, where the twinkling lights of the stars and moon shade like diamonds over its clear skies, where roses and flowers are spread all over its fields like precious stones in the heart of green shells, where butterflies play the hide-and-seek game with the gentle breeze, and where the animals gather to drink from the sweet water of the river. I was forged with this lovely nature of Lebanon, where only in here we have the gift of the four seasons, the high mountains with the white ornaments, and a shore calming with arms wide open the angry waves of the sea. [18, p4]

Generations later, in America, as I followed the family journey, I tried to understand the motivation for the Raad emigration and that of so many other Lebanese families, her words ring so true:

In 1895, my parents left this village 'Lebaa,' in the east of Saida City in South Lebanon, heading to America because of the bad economic situation caused by the repeated wars on this land. People found themselves without jobs or work. They felt so frustrated that some left to Brazil and others to America. My parents loved Lebaa so much, that they even took me with them as I was only 2 years old, and left my 6 years old sister Barbara (nee Nahra) at my uncle Tannous' house, to keep a connection with their homeland. It was also to keep one member of the family alive in the occasion anything bad happened to the rest of the family while traveling by sea, being the only way to travel back in these days. After a long two months of traveling in the sea, we arrived in America (South America) and stayed for some time in Buenos Aries, where my father opened a grocery store and it was a good business. My mother gave birth to a beautiful little girl named Sarah, and we loved her so much. We left Buenos Aires and moved to George Town. [18, p4]

Helen shares with us that her grandmother's elder sister Barbara grew up and married her cousin Tannous Youssef (Thomas Joseph) in the church in Lebaa. Shortly thereafter, Thomas and Barbara Joseph left Lebaa to join brother Nicholas in Georgetown to begin the family business of N. Joseph & Brother.

An interesting anecdote that she shares offers one of the similarities between tiny Lebaa and little Georgetown. Helen explains that the marriage was performed by a priest Youssef Kassem, who rode his horse from a nearby village to perform the ceremony. You will learn in another chapter that a similar Catholic arrangement was in place in Georgetown in the 1800s. It had no Catholic Church until 1902 and the only Catholic services and masses were performed by priests riding "circuit" in the missionary south and arriving by horseback. Nicholas and Aneesie would be the first couple to become married in the new Church in Georgetown, S.C.

Helen's grandmother Elizabeth remained in Georgetown from age three until she was 18 years old. Her parents decided that an "arranged marriage" to a Lebanese family member back in Lebaa was what they wanted for their daughter. It was decided that she would return to Lebaa and she would be married to Tobias, the son of Youssef. Helen offers a tearful remembrance by her grandmother:

> *I cried so much when I heard his words and I prayed a lot for my parents to refuse. I was frightened to live in a land that I didn't remember. Of the World War I that was on, of being with someone I never met or saw… My sister Barbara was the only one who felt my pain, because she went through the same when my parents left her to go to America, her being only a child.* [18, p5]

It would not be until 1962 that Helen's grandmother Elizabeth would return to America where she had come as a 2-year-old and was sent back to marry as an 18-year-old.

RAAD/JOSEPH FAMILY TREE AND REUNIONS

I was late to the party. I did not get introduced into the Raad/Joseph family reunions until the 1990s but, oh what an introduction and what a lasting impression. But let's start at the beginning. There could only be reunions if there was a strong family bond and a large number of willing participants. It is fun to recount where it all started and who is related to whom.

The Family Tree

There is an enormous rolled up document in our house in Georgetown that traces the Raad Family tree back some 350 years. The branches are many and reach far and wide: Lebanon, Syria, Europe, Asia, North and South America, Cuba. It was prepared by Dr. Maroun Raad and first presented to the family by Helen Raad Bou-Karam in 2009.

The Georgetown branch of the tree can be traced to four brothers: Nicholas, Thomas, Shickory, and John. The four brothers had 20 children and 65 grandchildren. They and their many offspring are the focus of this work. The brothers all came to Georgetown, South Carolina. All four brothers prospered. All loved family, God and their adopted America. *Those Joseph parents… were strict in terms of instilling principles that would guide the younger ones into their responsibilities in the business community and Christian worlds. Those guidelines set down by the parents are still applicable to the lives of their children and their children's children as they follow their set courses.* [22, p6-B]

Among the children and grandchildren were prosperous business owners, professionals, academics and bankers. They, as a group, did much in the 100 years of the 20th century in Georgetown to shape the community, the schools, their beloved Catholic church. From personal experience, I can attest to the fact that their greatest achievement was in the strong family values instilled in the succeeding generations. Their daily lives exemplify it. Their reunions revel in it. As Ethlyn Missroon in the *Georgetown Times* put it: *… two or three generations of the family… good-looking people who know how to laugh and enjoy life and still contribute to their communities as serious citizens.* [22, p6-B]

My wife is in the second generation. Her father was Alfred Joseph and his dad was John Joseph. As you will see from the summary of the family below, it is impossible to cover them all. What I have done is to try to set their emigration to America in the context of what they as a people went through, how little they had when they arrived, and how critical it was to have other Lebanese around them to support and nurture their spirit. They ventured to foreign lands, often having to stay for a time in different countries. They arrived with many challenges: no money, meager English language skills, dark skins, and their unpopular Maronite-Catholic faith. But, they came determined to make a better life for themselves and their children. Now, more than a hundred years later, it is clear that they excelled in their quest, prospered in the journey and left a legacy of love, pride and contributions to Georgetown and to their adopted country.

The only way I knew to cover the four brother's families was to provide anecdotes from each to give you a sense of the wonder of how four brothers could create such a legacy:

- Pop, the football star on "The Big Train, 1939 Winyah Gators High School team"
- The Dental Dynasty of dozens of dentists among the Josephs
- Front Street merchants with all four families setting up business after business
- The legendary Thomas Café still serving meals almost 80 years after its start
- St. Mary's parish at the heart of this family of believers

I have sprinkled into each section vignettes that attempt to capture the uniqueness of these families and the power of the love they have for each other and that they so willingly shared with those they came in contact with.

The Reunions

"One of the reasons for having our family reunion is that you will know one another and continue to keep in contact with one another. A second reason is to keep us aware of our heritage." [27, p1]

It was through the family reunions that I first got a chance to savor this extraordinary family in all of its glory. About 75 years after the four brothers began to arrive in America, the clan decided they should try to bring the extended family together. By the mid-1970s they numbered above 100 and many were still right in Georgetown or in South Carolina. The reunion would be a chance for disparate grandchildren of the four progenitors to either meet for the first time or to reacquaint.

They would bring along the Catholic priests who had helped nurture their faith. They would dress in their finest and of course they would do what all immigrant families do; they would revel in their favorite family foods. To those of us who had married into the clan, we would marvel at their savory tabbouleh, fattoush, hummus, baba ghanoush, kibbeh and Sambusac. On the serious side, there would be prayer and speeches and opportunities for elders to recount the family history, share a family tree or introduce a loved one who had traveled from the old country for the event. Over the next 40 years the clan would gather at least five times with the numbers eventually reaching 250 as the fifth generation took their cherished places (great and great great grandchildren). The first reunion in 1974 and the most recent one in 2011 provide a sense of the wonder of these gatherings.

The first Raad/Joseph Reunion was held on the weekend of June 29-30 in 1974. It was held at the Sea Gull Inn, Georgetown. In attendance were 103 Josephs along with three of the favorite St. Mary former priests: Reverend Albert A. Faase and the Reverend Joseph Maher. Sunday Mass was offered by Monsignor Richard Madden. In a *Georgetown Times* article, it was pointed out that these three were known within the family as the "Lebanese priests" because of their friendship with all of the Joseph family. It was at this reunion that an elaborate painting of the family tree with all the descendants of Joseph Thomas Raad in America listed. It was also at this first reunion that Kelly Khoury and his wife Angel were "adopted" into the Joseph clan. They went on to become integral members of the family.

An even larger family reunion, as promised, was held in July of 1979. Once again at the Sea Gull. This reunion attracted the attention of the *Georgetown Times* and a number of the quotes are worth repeating:

> *A great gathering recently of a joyous Georgetown family by the original name of Joseph underlines one of the most important of American maxims and postures: patriotism, love of country and family. And further… that America is the land of opportunity for those who have the wit and wisdom to judiciously avail themselves of what this land has to offer.* [22, p6-B]

Reunions were held in Camden in 1988, in Pawleys Island in 1993 and most recently in 2011 with 250 plus in attendance. With many of the second generation in their 80s and 90s and others sadly already passed away, the third generation is planning the next reunion for late 2017/2018. You can only wish that you could come and revel in the magic.

The reunions and the work on this book have helped to spark a new project: The Georgetown Lebanese Legacy Project. The project was conceived and is being driven by the Georgetown County Public Library and its very capable staff. Oral histories of the Lebanese families, especially second and third generation are being videotaped. Interviews are being conducted. Artifacts and old photos are being catalogued. With a grant from the South Carolina Humanities Council, a year end multi-day event is being planned at which a documentary on the families will be released, photos and artifacts will be showcased and a panel of historians, authors and immigration scholars will place the work in context. The Library Project is doing its work in conjunction with North Carolina State University and its Lebanese Diaspora Studies Center. The Georgetown Project will be set up as a traveling exhibit to be made available to libraries and museums throughout the State and South. We know that there will be keen interest especially in those cities and towns like Camden and Columbia and Summerton with vibrant Lebanese descendent communities.

John Kenny

A Very Special Family

N. JOSEPH & BROTHER
The First Joseph Business in Georgetown

In 1902, Nicholas Joseph and Thomas Joseph, sons of Thon Raad Joseph and Mary Habib, opened their dry goods business on the first floor in the buildings located at 701 and 703 Front Street. In Lebanon, their names were Nahreh Raad and Tannous Raad. But, like so many immigrants, their names were often converted, either by the immigration authorities, or by themselves to easy sounding "Americanized" names, both first and last. Thus, each of the Raad brothers and their families in the U.S. would forever be known as the Josephs. Nicholas was the oldest of the four Joseph boys, all of whom were born in Lebanon. Nicholas in 1873, Thomas in 1885, Shickory in 1887 and John in 1889.

This picture of the N. Joseph and Brother store in the early 1900s shows the breadth of the goods offered. The partnership of the two brothers remained until 1931 when it became T. Joseph and Sons grocery and milk store where sons of Thomas – David, Nimmer, John and Paul – often worked and were later joined by their sisters, Zion, Helen and Pauline. Over the 71 years of continuous operation by the Joseph family, T. Joseph and Sons would evolve to become Joseph's Lucky Dollar Store, Lucky $ and United Finance. In addition to the businesses run there, many of the Joseph families lived in the apartments above the stores. These were pre-hospital days and many of the first generation Josephs were born there. John A. Joseph, Sr. was born there in 1916 and eventually opened his first dentist office there after returning from World War II. In 1931, the building at 703 was taken over by Nicholas's wife, Aneesie, and then in 1932 it was rented to Escie Thomas.

John Kenny

NICHOLAS RAAD JOSEPH and THOMAS RAAD JOSEPH
2 Brothers, 1 Family Unit: 11 Kids and 42 Grandkids

This is an incredible saga of two brothers so closely bound that they left their homeland, their brothers, sisters and parents and built a business together in the new world, in Georgetown, S.C. They lived in the same home together. Married childhood brides, each in their teens and between them fathered 11 children, bearing 42 grandchildren. Nicholas would only live until 1920, while Thomas lived twenty years more and died in 1940. They worked hard. Cared passionately about family. Loved God and their newly adopted country. Nicholas was the first to come to America. Shortly thereafter, he returned to Lebanon and returned with brother Thomas and his two stepbrothers, Shickory and John, and brought them to their new homeland.

I had the good fortune to interview at length and on multiple occasions three of Thomas and Barbara Joseph's 7 children (Helen, Paul and Pauline) after moving to Georgetown in 2011. I also had met Zion long before starting this research, but never knew John, Nimmer or David. My loss. I lived in Georgetown, as did Helen and therefore got to know her quite well. I traveled to Charleston to spend time with Pauline and eventually traveled up to Camden to visit Paul and learned of the immense Joseph clan in that beautiful city. David and Paul had homes next to each other and each fathered 8 children and had a passel of grandkids. Only their sister Zion had outdone them. She had nine kids and even more grandkids. Needless to say, this was a prolific and fertile family.

Unfortunately, I never got to interview any of Nicholas and Aneesie Joseph's four children, Arthur, Kellie, Joseph or Victoria. I had met Arthur and his wife Bert years earlier and knew them to be true characters and assets to the Georgetown community. Because Nicholas died in 1920, the Nicholas and Aneesie family lived with Thomas and Barbara, and the families were essentially merged. This meant that Thomas, Barbara and Aneesie raised 11 children together and jointly ran their businesses side by side or in some case commingled. It is for that reason, I have combined the stories of Nicolas and Thomas into a single section.

The interviews with each of the three first generation children of Thomas and Barbara in their 80s and 90s was nothing short of charming and life-affirming. Each was ecstatic to think about a family history being captured and maybe published, and each was prepared to offer family history, anecdotes and to share the pure familial love that was part and parcel of these 53 first- and second-generation Josephs. Later, you will learn how two of the first generation Thomas children built a lake house together that could sleep more than 50 adults and children, and often did.

In 2013, Paul, Helen and Pauline pulled together a special luncheon at the Rice Paddy Restaurant in Georgetown with family members from the 2nd, 3rd, and 4th generation. It was wondrous. Stories abounded. Memories filled the room. Ninety-year-old siblings corrected their youngest sister, only in her 80s, for facts "mis-remembered." Their stories were better than any novel or Broadway play.

- "Who was really born above the dry goods store?"
- "Did Dr. John really have his first dental office there?"
- "Did the bells of the town clock really strike midnight as the youngest child was being born at home?"

This after all was a special family. Also in attendance were three of Thomas and Barbara's grandchildren: John Joseph, Jr., Barbara Dumm, and Helen Chia. My wife Mary Lou, granddaughter of John Joseph, was also in attendance.

NICHOLAS RAAD JOSEPH

Born in Lebaa, Lebanon approximately (1873 and died 1920)
Came to America at age 27
He was the first brother to come to America and returned to Lebaa to bring his brothers: Thomas, Shickory and John
Married to Aneesie Nahra (born 1884 and died 1959)

They had 4 children:
    Kellie Joseph
    Victoria Inez Joseph
    Joseph Joseph
    Arthur Joseph, married to Bertha Carter Joseph

Nicholas and Aneesie had 7 grandchildren:
    Kellie had one child:
        Lynn
    Joseph's children:
        Joseph, Jr.
        Mary Jo
    Arthur's children:
        Joye Ann Joseph Deane
        Nicholas Raad Joseph
        Jackson Carter Joseph
        Victoria Carter Meredith

Nicholas and Aneesie had a number of great grandchildren.

A Very Special Family

VIGNETTE: THE NICHOLAS JOSEPH FAMILY
By Carter Joseph

"Sit-tee" – Aneesie Nahra Joseph

My "Sit-tee" (paternal grandmother) had the most adorable accent, as did all of our grandparents who moved to Georgetown from Lebanon. English was her second language, learned the hard way, and filtered through the distinct accent of coastal South Carolina. From her lovely mouth, the word *"y'all"* acquired two extra syllables. Of all her grandchildren, she cherished the firstborn, Joye Anne. She was known to say, *"I love all my grandchildren, but Jai-Yann's my honey."*

Whenever she would welcome us, her beloved grandchildren, she would throw open her arms and cry out in joy, *"Ya hon-ney, ya dar-lin' ya muhaluck!"* (What '*muhaluck*' meant was anyone's guess, but we knew it was a term of endearment.) The master bedroom suite on the first floor of that lovely house on Prince Street was rented out to Ms. Bertha Blanchard, lady friend of the esteemed Rene Cathou, proprietor of the fresh seafood market on the docks of St. James Street.

Every Friday, Sit-tee would make her unleavened bread, which she called *"tin bread."* Whether she was trying to say "thin bread" is beside the point. The bread was baked on round tins that had held the reels of films at the movie theater. She had acquired a few of those. As I stood transfixed in her kitchen, she would take the balls of dough and throw them up in the air, catching and shaping them on the way down. After five tosses or so, they formed perfect thin circles, about fifteen inches in diameter. To this day, I make her tabbouleh and mugrabeeyeh, the hearty soup made from a whole chicken, onions, tiny semolina balls, and chickpeas. And they don't turn out too badly, either.

From Lebanon, she had brought a cutting of the fig tree from her home. It had turned into a noble fruit tree in her backyard, so we had an unending supply of large, succulent, sweet figs, the likes of which I have not tasted since. And hanging on the clothes line was a dripping cloth bag, making the week's supply of lubbin, the Lebanese yogurt, for which the active culture was always kept. Food is love.

She was about five feet tall and wore her hair in a bun in the back. When very young, I used to bathe with her in the tub, and can remember a small rose tattoo above her left breast. When I turned five, her health began to fade, and she could no longer negotiate the steep steps to the second floor. Miss Bertha reluctantly had to move upstairs.

My first encounter with real heartbreak occurred at age six, when Sit-tee died. Because I was so young, I was not allowed to attend her funeral, for fear that I would cry and make a scene, though I promised I would behave. Still, I felt cheated, stayed behind at her house, and bawled all afternoon.

Sit-tee had four children. The eldest, Kellie became a doctor, a lung specialist, thanks to the largesse of Uncle Nimmer. He married a cold, ill-tempered woman and set up practice in her far-away home town, Birmingham. Uncle Kelly remains in my memory as learned, sophisticated, exceedingly kind, and quite witty. His many letters were like visits, despite his doctor's handwriting. When we moved into our new home in the early '60s, Uncle Kellie sent us a plaque which remained in the dining area of Mama's state-of-the-art kitchen. It stated, "The Opinions Expressed by the Husband in This House are Not Necessarily those of the Management."

The second child was my adored Aunt Victoria, about whom you will learn more.

Next was Joseph Nicholas Joseph, the macho body-builder. When Uncle Joe was a teen, the circus came to town. The "strong man" of the traveling entourage challenged any local who was brave enough to fight him to bring it on. Sure enough, Uncle Joe whipped his ass and became a family legend. He soon moved to Baltimore and married lovely Aunt Mary. How's this for being Catholic: Young couple Mary and Joseph (Joseph). He worked at Bethlehem Steel. And they lived on Church Road.

The baby of the family was my father, Arthur. No middle name. My grandfather died shortly after Papa's birth, the cause of which, sadly I do not know. So, Sit-tee moved her family into the Kaminski Street home of her sister Auntie Barbara and her husband Uncle Thomas, my grandfather's brother. Twelve children in that boisterous, joyful home! But that is another story.

A Very Special Family

Papa – Arthur Joseph

Daddy was the baby of his family, and always retained a child-like sense of happiness. He loved a good time, a good drink, a good game of golf, and had no enemies. Short in stature, gentle in nature, and really handsome, he had a way with the ladies, and was known as "The Mouse" or "The Little Dynamo."

Many Sunday afternoons, Uncle Tom would load the entire extended family into the big truck, like the Joads in *The Grapes of Wrath* (although Lebanese), and make sure the tank was full. They would point the car and just drive in any direction, in the country or to the beach, just for the fun of the outing. Before the fuel reached the halfway mark, they would turn around and return home. Once they were having such a good time that Papa, about five years old, asked Uncle Tom why they were going back to Georgetown so soon. After all, there was still more than half a tank of gas left. Uncle Tom replied, "Let me tell you something, Kid Joe. The last half goes the fastest!" A valuable lesson indeed.

During World War Two, Daddy was stationed in northern Africa, southern Italy, and Sicily. He fell in love with a gorgeous Sicilian girl named Gigiola. When the war was over and as he was shipped back home, he promised to send for her. Then he met Bert Carter, and it was addio, Gigiola. Aunt Vic had met my mother while they both were nurses at International Paper, and a mutual friend, Benedict Lewenthal, arranged the first date.

My parents had a great courtship, double-dating with Uncle Johnny and his girlfriend Arlene (who looked like Dinah Shore), John and Liz Heinemann, Bubba Joe Cathou and Carol Jean, Mabel and Tommy Seale, Mary Agnes and Francis King, John and Helen Assey, Sylvan and Erma Rosen, Julius and Rita Fogel, and other unique Georgetown couples; great people and lifelong friends.

One night on a boating date to North Island on Winyah Bay with ten others, things got a bit out of hand. Raymond Moore fell overboard, but the men saved him. Mama caught her new pants on a nail and ripped them wide open. When they arrived at her home at 1 a.m., there was her stern father Jackson Carter standing at the door, scowling like J. Edgar Hoover. Fortunately, he didn't see the torn pants, and Mama told him in the dark as she tiptoed to her room not to worry, she had just gotten a little wet on the boat. Half-drunk, Daddy quietly returned to the car and high-tailed it home.

My Southern Baptist mother defied her judgmental, bigoted father and married this damned Catholic, and an A-Rab at that! Not looking back, she converted, because "mixed marriages" were not allowed by Holy Mother Church. That was a scandal for the Carter family and the community at large. The entire Lebanese clan embraced Mama as one of their own, the two cultures blended, and barriers melted away. So my parents were sort of a pivotal couple in town.

There's an old nursery rhyme: *"Jack Spratt could eat no fat, his wife could eat no lean. And so between them both, you see, they licked the platter clean."* That's Bert and Arthur in a nutshell. Opposites attract. They were fire and water, salt and pepper, sweet and salty. And they made quite a go of it.

They married on Christmas Day in 1945, at Sit-tee's home, the reception courtesy of Aunt Vic. Mama's parents stayed away, but the rest of her family were there. (Because Christmas swallows everything in its path, like a hurricane, most years their wedding anniversary went by barely noticed, except for sister Joye and Aunt Vic.) Within four years, there were three children, so the honeymoon was extremely short, and the realities of rearing a family set in.

They bought a house on Queen Street, Daddy started a beer distributorship, opened a liquor store, and worked many 18-hour days. Even when he got home around midnight, there was always a hot meal ready for him. He was a savvy businessman, found out how money works, realized that beer was too labor-intensive for

A Very Special Family

the profits earned, sold it off, bought another liquor store. We were well-provided for, and had an idyllic childhood on Queen Street in the 1950s. Then sister Vicky arrived, and we moved.

When color TV became the standard, Daddy held out, claiming that "It's not perfected yet," despite my incessant pleading. When our ancient Philco black-and-white finally died, it was time. I insisted on an RCA, but he bought a damned Zenith to save $20. Papa resembled the great Jack Benny in more than one way, and could squeeze a dollar until it cried for mercy.

Three decades later, at their new home in Wedgefield, I was visiting from Atlanta when their most recent TV gave out. So I went to Wal-Mart, bought a state-of-the-art big-screen Toshiba, brought it home and set it up. He was completely amazed and delighted at the picture quality. Giving him a big kiss on his bald dome, I proudly said, "Pop, they PERFECTED it at last! Enjoy!"

Daddy's interests were business and sports, shared by my brother Nick, and I admit to having no affinity for either of these. If Nick was the son you wanted, I was the son you got, and loved without reservation. However, Papa and I loved the great Warner Brothers cartoons. Once, while changing channels, I stopped on Bugs Bunny. When it was over, Daddy looked at me and said, "Son, I always thought you would end up doing something like that for a living. You know, if you had moved to New York or California, I would have supported you until you got on your feet. Should I have told you?" After I picked up my jaw from the floor, I took a deep breath, and said, "Pop, I would have really liked to have known. But if I had done that, I would probably be dead by now. And you always did the best you could." Again, I gave him a big kiss. What a dear, dear man.

Another time, Mama was giving him hell about something or other, which he endured without a hint of annoyance. She said, "I'll show him. I'm going to spend every last bit of his money!" With a self-satisfied, greatly amused gleam in his eye, he said to me, "She couldn't do it if she tried."

Toward the end, I asked him how he was feeling, and the answer was, "About as well as I can for the shape I'm in." That's Papa. He never complained once. If you asked Mama the same question, you were going to know the entire answer, and then some.

Aunt Vic – Victoria Irene Joseph

My Aunt Victoria Irene was the kindest woman I have ever known, and the best friend I ever had. Her love was unconditional and completely accepting, with a generosity of spirit that asked for nothing in return. A nurse by profession and by vocation, she had twice been named Catholic Nurse of the Year by the Diocese of Charleston. Her specialty was ministering to seasonal migrant workers, mostly from Mexico. Although she spoke no Spanish, her language of mercy and care was universally understood.

Aunt Vic practiced in Charleston and lived in a little townhouse on Trapman Street in the center of that beautiful, traffic-clogged city. Most weekends she would travel to Georgetown to be with us, staying at Sit-tee's house, arriving Friday evening and leaving after Sunday dinner. Usually she would be bearing gifts; the latest fashions for my mother and sisters, sporting goods for my brother, art supplies and books for me. She took great delight in my meager talents in drawing, and was unfailing in her encouragement.

During adolescence, I sometimes spent weekends with her in Charleston. In young adulthood, I would visit her from Atlanta occasionally. During the first Spoleto festivals, I took her to classical recitals and the occasional opera, which delighted her no end.

In the early 1960s she and Uncle Isaac E. Isaac made a pilgrimage to Lebanon, the old country. They were feted and treated like royalty. She brought me back an Arabian head gear and black robe trimmed with faux gold that made me look like a shiek.

In the early 1970s we went on a 10-day tour of Italy together – her treat. I was her tour guide to Florence and Rome. (This was my second trip, so I knew the territory.) When we arrived at our hotel in Florence, I left to get some brochures. When I got back, she looked just a bit flustered and told me that there had been a power outage, and she had been stuck in the elevator for an hour. As I freaked out, she told me to calm down. She said that she just prayed, knew God would take care of her, and that she was fine. Now that's what I call unflinching faith.

Our last day was at the Vatican. We left very early in the morning and toured the endless galleries. Since most of these masterful paintings were of Biblical subjects that she knew well, I would point out the finer aspects of their craftsmanship, and explain what made them great art.

Last stop was the interior of St. Peter's Basilica, and we were both overwhelmed. At the end of this glorious day, as we left the Catholic Church's epicenter, we turned for a final look at St. Peter's Square. The arms of Michelangelo's and Bernini's magnificent portico seemed to reach out to embrace us, and she stopped. With tears of joy, she trembled a bit, grabbed my hand and said, "Honey, this has been the most wonderful day of my life!" Mine too, Aunt Vic, and all because of you. Right then the last bus pulled up, and we had only a few seconds to board or be stranded. I literally picked her up and deposited her little body inside the bus, hopped on, and off we went into the dusk.

Aunt Vic left us far too soon, in her mid-fifties. After an ill-advised year in Florida, I got word that she was ill. Packing up my things, I was rushing to Charleston to take care of her. To my eternal regret, by the time I got there, she was gone. Not a day goes by that I do not think of her with great love and gratitude. If I could choose my family, it would be the one I have. We could not be more blessed.

THOMAS RAAD JOSEPH

Born in Lebaa, Lebanon (b.1885 and died 1940)
Came to America at age 15 to be with his brother Nicholas
    And was joined by John and Shickory
Married to Barbara Nahra (b. 1892 and died 1965)

They had 7 children:
    John Anthony Joseph, m. Arlene Wilcox
    Nimmer Joseph, m. Rosalee Sheheen
    Helen Joseph, m. John Francis Walsh
    Zion Joseph, m. George Henry Amann
    David Joseph, m. Rose Mary Sayeg
    Paul Joseph, m. Margaret Shadid
    Pauline Joseph, m. Vincent Nicholas Sottile, Sr.

John, Nimmer, David, Paul

A Very Special Family

Thomas and Barbara had 35 grandchildren

John Joseph's children:
- Thomas Joseph
- John Joseph
- Raad Joseph

Nimmer Joseph's children:
    Mary Ann Joseph Lumpkin
    James Joseph

Helen Joseph's children:
    Carol Ann Walsh Asay
    John Francis Walsh, Jr.
    Michael Anthony Walsh
    Trudy Elizabeth Walsh

A Very Special Family

Zion Joseph's children:
- George Paul Amann
- Barbara Elizabeth Amann Dumm
- Helen Marie Amann Chiha
- Mary Jo Amann Karre
- Sarah Nahra Amann Chiha
- Rebecca Ann Amann
- Joseph John Amann, Sr.
- Paul Vincent Amann
- Albert Anthony Amann

David Joseph's children:
- Jan Theresa Ross
- David Thomas Joseph, Jr.
- Kathy Ann Joseph Hutchinson
- Rosemary Joseph Olano
- Robin Marie Joseph
- Robert Michael Joseph
- Kellie Nahra Joseph Byrnes
- Timothy Gerard Joseph

Paul Joseph's children:
- Karen Joseph Theos
- Ellen Joseph Cherof
- Pauline Joseph Frampton
- Mary Joseph Hayes
- Margaret Joseph Koutroulakis
- Libby Joseph Wullner
- Paul Thomas Joseph, Jr.
- Michael Anthony Joseph

Pauline Joseph's children:
    Vincent Nicholas Sottile, Jr.
    Mary Sottile Regner

Thomas and Barbara had a whole bunch of great grandchildren!

A Very Special Family

VIGNETTE: JOHN ANTHONY JOSEPH
First of the Dental Dynasty
By Raad Joseph

John Anthony Joseph, Sr. was born to Thomas and Barbara Nahra Joseph on November 18, 1916 in Georgetown, S.C. Like so many deliveries at that time, John was born in the family home which was located above their family business on 701 Front Street. Prior to John's birth, Thomas and Barbara had three children: two who died during childbirth or shortly afterwards; the third, Olin Joseph, was born in October of 1914 and died at 2 years old of Broncho-pneumonia in January of 1916. The loss of Olin had a devastating effect on Thomas and Barbara, and Barbara prayed to God that if he would grant her a son who would live past childhood, she would name him after John the Baptist. Upon John's birth, she fulfilled her commitment. John was spoiled from birth and always held a special place in his mother's heart. Barbara would always recite an Arabic saying and prayer when being around children; blessing the children and also acknowledging that parents should never have to bury their children.

John attended public school in Georgetown and helped his father in the family business. T. Joseph and Sons was a grocery store and John delivered groceries, and often times accompanied his father selling groceries out of the back of their truck at various locations around Georgetown County. He often told his children stories of selling produce to the wealthier families who had homes on Pawleys Island. He declared that one day he also would have a home on the Island. John fulfilled that dream in 1968 at the age of 52.

Growing up in Georgetown was a happy time as there were many Lebanese people in the community, most of whom were related. And, even if you were not, if you were Lebanese, you were family. This is not to say that he and his family did not face challenges living in the South in the early 1900s. Born to immigrant parents who spoke broken English and of Catholic faith, the family experienced many prejudices. Still, the community embraced the family and for every person who looked down on the family, there were many more who treated them with respect. Unfortunately, these prejudices left a mark on John, and he spent his life trying to overcome the stigma.

John attended public school, graduated from Winyah High School in 1934 and went on to attend the University of South Carolina. After completion of his sophomore year, he applied and was accepted to Atlanta Southern Dental College which later became part of Emory University. John flourished in Dental school, participating in social and academic organizations and developing lifelong friends. Sadly, prior to starting his junior year, his father took ill and died. His father, knowing he was not going to live, made plans for his children and decided that John would stay in school, and Nimmer would look after the family with his mom and run the family business. John went on to finish Dental School in 1941.

Upon graduation, John set up practice in Myrtle Beach, S.C. It is still unclear why he chose Myrtle Beach. Speculation is that a close friend, Gabe Joseph, who was also Lebanese, but no relation, convinced him of the opportunity. In 1943, John was called to serve in World War II. He joined the Army Air Corp and was stationed at Bruning Army Airfield, just outside of Fairbury, Nebraska. As fate would have it, working in the dental clinic as a secretary was his future wife, Arlene Wilcox. Arlene, who had previously taught school upon graduation from Hastings College, took a job at the base during the summer as the pay was double what she was making teaching school.

John was six years older than Arlene, but in August of that year he convinced her to let him call on her. She lived off the base in Fairbury with her best friend and her friend's grandmother. They got along well and upon receiving news in November that he was going overseas, he and Arlene decided to get married. Several weeks later, John left for Italy where he served for 18 months, writing Arlene daily and sometimes two or three times a day.

In November of 1945, upon completion of his tour of duty and the surrender of Japan to end the War, John and Arlene moved back to Georgetown where he began his practice and their life together. His parents had since moved from over the store to a home on Hazzard Street, and John and Arlene briefly lived with them until they could find a place of their own. John started his practice in his family's previous home, above the family business on 701 Front Street and practiced there until he moved his practice across the street to 632 Front Street. John practiced in this location until he retired in 1995.

John and Arlene had three children together, Thomas born in 1946, John Jr. born in 1949 and Raad, born in 1955. He and Arlene were active in the community participating in several professional and social organizations. John, upon starting his practice in Georgetown, also helped to send his two brothers, David and Paul, to college and dental school and his sisters, Zion and Pauline, to college. John and Arlene both were also active in their churches: John continuing to support St. Mary's Catholic Church, where he was baptized and raised; Arlene supporting the Georgetown Presbyterian Church, the faith of her upbringing. In addition to their active life in Georgetown, they loved to travel and pretty much saw the world. Often times with friends, often times with their family, and they even travelled on several "Good Will" trips abroad with Governors West and McNair representing the State of South Carolina.

John passed away in 1996 but not before seeing his sons complete their education and start their families. He had the great fortune to see all six of his grandchildren born and lived long enough that they all have loving memories of their Gidee. John also had the great fortune to have his son John join him in his practice in 1997 and his nephew, Timothy Joseph, join the practice upon his retirement. Joseph Dental Associates is still operating at 632 Front Street. It is the longest commercial business operating on Front Street.

John died of cancer in 1996 and Arlene lived in Georgetown until her death in 2014 at 92. Although not of Lebanese descent, Arlene loved being called Sittee.

VIGNETTE: HELEN JOSEPH WALSH
From Interviews by her son Michael and his wife Lisa

In piecing together the Thomas and Nicholas history, I got a major boost from Helen who was interviewed by her son Michael and his wife Lisa.

Nicholas and Thomas Joseph Raad each came to America from Lebaa in Lebanon seeking a better life, arriving through Ellis Island in New York harbor, like millions of other immigrants. Helen, at 94, recalled that her parents had shared the story that, when Nicholas and Thomas arrived, they did not speak any English and had a name tag pinned onto their clothing to indicate who they were and that their destination was Georgetown, South Carolina in the U.S.A. Nicholas was in his 20's, but Thomas only fifteen or sixteen, and they traveled alone on a ship for days that had sailed out of the Mediterranean Sea across the vast Atlantic Ocean.

Oldest brother Nicholas was the first of the family to come to America. Within four years he was encouraging his younger brothers Thomas and John to join him. Perhaps Nicholas helped finance the trip. He did have a very great interest in their coming, as they were to bring and did bring the young Aneesie Nahra with them. Nicholas and Aneesie would become the first Catholic couple to be married in the new St. Mary's Catholic Church that opened its doors in 1902.

We learn from the history piece presented at a Joseph family reunion by Nicholas and Aneesie Joseph's daughter, Victoria Joseph, the following about Nicholas and their brothers:

> *He seems to have joined the group at the Kozmas, which now included Joseph and Wadia Masad Kosma, Joe's father-in-law, Assad Masad. Their first adventure was peddling. The men went, a few together, to a town where they rented space in a warehouse where they could leave their supply of commodities. They went*

A Very Special Family

out, going from door to door, with their items in a back pack. When all the goods were sold, they returned to Georgetown ready to stock up again and go back out on their rounds. [27, p2]

Peddling was an important aspect of rural life in the post-civil war period. Many former slaves and other former plantation workers chose to live on the land as subsistence farmers and did not care to travel to the city to purchase their staples. The Lebanese peddlers helped fill this need and of course earned both a living and the beginnings of savings to open businesses in town.

The two Joseph brothers must have been successful peddling, since they bought one building at 701 Front Street and eventually another at 703 Front Street. In 2017, these buildings still stand. It was at 701/703 that Nicholas and Thomas set up their dry goods store, N. Joseph and Brother. These buildings housed Lebanese businesses for the next fifty years; in one case, Thomas Café, (the subject of a separate chapter) for the next hundred years after their arrival in Georgetown. Thomas also saved enough to purchase a home on Prince Street where he raised his family of seven children. It was during this same period that Thomas Joseph's wife's parents, Paul and Helen Nahra, came to Georgetown and opened a general store.

The Joseph brothers' store on Front Street is wonderfully described by Victoria in her 1974 reunion presentation:

This store was a child's delight. Fruit, candy, Coca-Cola, cookies, parched peanuts, chewing gum in one part of the store; dry goods on the other side. You could buy yard cloth, overalls (not jeans), ribbon for the hair, socks, shirts, and what have you. Pay was incidental. If you could have peanuts, cookies and other goodies while working that was heaven to a small child and 25 cents to $1.00 for all day until midnight. You felt you were getting a good deal. There were no minimum wage laws. All that was required was being old enough or tall enough to reach the counter. [27, p3]

The oldest Joseph brother Nicholas died in 1920, 18 years after arriving in America. He left behind his widow, Aneesie, and their four children. It was younger brother Thomas and wife Barbara who stepped forward to take care of his brother's family. According to the family, it was Thomas who would transfer ownership of the 703 Front Street building and the home on Prince Street to Nicholas' widow, and it was he who would help send Nicholas' son Kellie to college and medical school and daughter Victoria to nursing school.

Thomas and his wife Barbara struggled in the early stages of their marriage to have children. Daughter Helen recounted in 2014 the trials of those first pregnancies. The story underscores both their determination as well as their faith in God:

Momma and Poppa lost three infant children early in their marriage. When Momma was pregnant the first time, she prayed to Saint John the Baptist, if you bless me with a healthy boy, I'll name him John. My grandmother, being a strong personality insisted on another name. The baby died. This happened two more times, and each time my grandmother won out in naming the baby and unfortunately both children died. Finally, with Momma's fourth pregnancy, she prayed to Saint John the Baptist that if this child lived, she would name him John. [44, p2]

John lived and went on to serve his country in the U.S. Air Force. It was he who was the first in the long line of Joseph dentists, which now number into the teens. (*See chapter on Dental Dynasty.*) Thomas and Barbara had six more healthy children. A wonderful story has become folklore in the Thomas Joseph family:

One day Momma (Barbara) was working in the grocery store when a prominent Georgetown lady stopped by the store after Christmas. She showed Momma a beautiful diamond ring her husband had given her for Christmas. She asked Momma if she could see her ring. Momma's ring was just a setting with a missing stone. She said to the woman: "Oh, you want to see my diamonds, well look around the store, there's Johnny, and Nimmer, and Helen, and David, and Paul and Pauline. There are my diamonds. [44, p3]

Thomas died at age 54 and Barbara was left a widow to raise the seven children. The older children were at critical stages of their education, but it appeared they would need to work in the newly opened International Paper Mill. Barbara was having none of it. She insisted that oldest son John graduate from high school and attend the University of South Carolina and eventually attend Dental School in Atlanta.

Thomas and his brother Nicholas were extremely close. In addition to buying the two buildings on Front Street where they ran their dry goods store, which eventually became a grocery store. The two brothers also bought a home on Prince Street, just a few blocks away. Both families lived in the same home. When Nicholas died, it was Thomas and Barbara who supported both his widow, Aneesie, and their four children along with their own seven children. Aneesie remained at home caring for the children, while Thomas and Barbara ran the store.

Thomas and Barbara eventually transferred one of the two Front Street buildings and the Prince Street home to Aneesie. Thomas and Barbara moved their family and lived above their store at 701 Front Street. Their son John, upon returning from World War II, would set up a dental practice in that location before building his dental office across the street, where his son John Jr. and nephew, Timothy continue to practice to this day. Eventually, they would help send Kellie to college and on to medical school and start him on his career as a lung specialist. Similarly, they helped to put their niece Victoria through nursing school and their nephew, Arthur through college.

The Great Depression created untold hardship throughout the world. Georgetown was no exception. The toll of destroyed lives, unemployment, failed businesses and starvation is nothing short of staggering. It was during the Depression that Thomas and Barbara sold their dry goods business and converted their store at 701 Front Street to groceries. The Depression was a severe, worldwide economic downturn that began with the U.S. Stock Market crash in September of 1929 and lasted until the middle of the 1940s. Like so many immigrant businesses in the 20th century, all children in the family were expected to work in their family's businesses. When Thomas died in 1940, it would be wife Barbara and her children who would continue to manage the store and eventually start new businesses all along Front Street. Helen and Paul were teenagers and along with their mother, they became the major bread winners for their family of eight. Helen, at age 94, shared some interesting anecdotes:

> *I was fine with managing the store, until a specialty rep came in to ask to see the manager. Since I was only 17, I was embarrassed to admit that I was the manager, so I would send the man back to the meat market*

to ask for Nimmer… he would then send the rep back up front to talk to me! My brother David was about 14 when he worked in the meat market. He would have to stand on a Coca Cola crate to wait on people. Our store backed up to the Sampit River. We had a lot of boaters shop in the store. One of the boaters came in the store and asked David if he could see the butcher. David, said, "I'm the butcher." The man couldn't believe his ears. He asked, "What do you know about cutting meat?" David said, "Tell me what you want, and I'll show you." Needless to say, the man was thoroughly impressed! [44, p3]

World War II, like the Great Depression, was the next trauma that the family had to cope with. Nimmer received a deferment as the head of the household while brother John joined the Air Force. David would find himself truly in harm's way. When the war broke out, he was 18. He immediately joined the Navy where he was attached to the U.S. Marine Corps 3rd Division. He was one of the courageous U.S. troops who fought at the bloody battle on Iwo Jima.

The Joseph brothers all believed in the importance of education in their children's lives. Thomas was no exception. John, David and Paul all became dentists. Pauline attended Columbia College and earned a degree in education. I recount in the "Dental Dynasty" chapter the wonderful story of how Paul and David got admitted to Georgetown University with the aid of the "Lebanese Family Priests" and the tenacity of older brother Nimmer. Support of the family's education was truly a family affair:

When Johnny went into dental practice after the war, Momma said to Johnny, "Your brother and sister, Helen and Nimmer, working in the family store, sent you to college, now it's your responsibility to educate your brother David." In the meantime, Nimmer and Helen worked in the store to also send Paul and Pauline to college. David attended America's oldest Catholic College, Georgetown University in Washington, D.C. He went into private dental practice after graduation, and Momma made him responsible for the remainder of Paul's dental education at Georgetown. Finally Pauline graduated from high school, and Nimmer and Helen assumed the responsibility of educating her as well. After Pauline completed two years of education, Helen got married and Nimmer continued to support Pauline during her last 2 years of education. [44, p4]

Another constant in the Lebanese families of Georgetown was their entrepreneurial drive. Everyone ran some sort of business to support their family. Helen and Zion were no exceptions. After sacrificing to help put her brothers and sisters through college, Helen married and moved to Greenwood with her husband.

She was not happy without her family and wanted to return home. Because of her sacrifice for her family's education, her brothers wanted to put her in a position to have a successful life in Georgetown. Because she gave them a future, they felt it was payback time and wanted to help her. They financed the opening of Delta Drug Sundries on Front Street in Georgetown with the understanding that if it failed, she owed them nothing. But, being a determined person, Helen worked hard along with her husband Red to run a successful business for almost 50 years. This included working her children in the store just as her mother had taught her to do. [44, p5]

Thomas and Barbara's fourth child, Zion, and her husband George had nine children. David and Paul would each have eight children. Even though George had a good job, raising nine children was a daunting task financially. Zion's brothers learned that she was talented in arranging flowers and suggested that she open a floral shop with their backing. She agreed and ran a successful business for more than thirty years.

A hundred years later, the people of Georgetown have fond memories of the many florist, grocery, card, pharmacy and other shops that the Joseph families built and ran in the city. They were, and are today, part and parcel of the entrepreneurial fabric of this wonderful port city.

VIGNETTE: ZION VERONICA JOSEPH AMANN
Mother of 9, Storekeeper, Mt. Zion
By Barbara Amann Dumm, her daughter

My mother was the fourth child in a brood of seven born to Thomas Raad Joseph and Barbara Nahra Joseph in January of 1924. By all accounts, she was the feisty one of the crew. Zion was named after her father's mother. I once looked up the meaning of the name, and it sure was appropriate, meaning *Monument, raised up or sepulcher built in stone.* Even in her early days, she was very strong willed. Her brother, Nimmer, the second oldest of the seven, took on the responsibility of running the family business and sending all of his siblings to college to further their education. There was a brother studying to be a dentist in Atlanta, sisters studying to be nurses, and others running businesses. Various first cousins were in dental and nursing schools. Education meant a great deal to this first generation of Josephs.

After graduating from Winyah High School in Georgetown, Zion was off to Charleston and St. Francis School of Nursing. A number of other Joseph family members had already attended and graduated from the school. It would become an early test of principle and will for the school and Zion. The young student noticed at St. Francis that the physicians, registered nurses and staff were all eating high off the hog compared to the nursing students. So, Mt. Zion rose up. She protested outside of the hospital to call attention to this discriminatory slight. The next phone call was painful. The Dean, not necessarily an easy going liberal, but more likely a tried and true Roman Catholic nun

A Very Special Family

or Mother Superior, summoned brother Nimmer to come pick her up. She was expelled. This was the 1940s and not the '60s.

Upon returning to Georgetown, with both principle and tail between her legs, Zion would begin her new life. George had first spotted Zion at the King's Arcade on Pawleys Island. He learned that she was part of the Joseph family in Georgetown and that he might find her again at the Lebanese run Thomas' Café on Front Street. He was right, the daughter of the owners was a cousin and friend of Zion. Louise Thomas Joseph introduced her to the man that would become the love of her life and the father of their nine children. George was stationed at the U.S. Air Force base in Charleston but would come to the airfield in Georgetown to act as an air traffic controller for Air Force pilots out of Charleston practicing touch-and-go landings. Zion knew right away that *He Was The One*. George Amann was neither Lebanese, nor Southern. He was of German ancestry and was raised in New York. In keeping with her feisty, should I say, impulsive nature, I'm told that Zion took a trip up to Staten Island to visit her new boyfriend and, while there, placed a call to her older brother Nimmer to inform him that she wasn't coming home. Rather, she was going to marry George. Nimmer insisted that she couldn't marry without Joseph family member representation at the wedding. Zion told him that she didn't care. She was in love and would marry him anyway. To her credit, she at least agreed to hold off long enough for Nimmer and other Joseph family to head north. The couple had a small wedding at George's mother's house with George in a suit and boutonniere and Zion in a suit and corsage. Her new life had begun.

George must have recognized early that Zion was very close to her very large Joseph family in Georgetown. In addition, he loved Georgetown and the lowcountry. It wasn't long before she convinced George to relocate from New York to South Carolina and her hometown.

For the first fifteen years of her marriage, Mama seemed to be pregnant with a new child every year or other year, eventually having nine children, five girls and four boys, and 21 grandchildren. She chose not to work outside the home, until her second oldest child was in the 12th grade. For 18 years, family and church were her passion. The stories are memorable. God and faith were daily parts of the family life. No family member would ever miss weekly Mass at St. Mary's. The Family Rosary was said each evening. Mama and Daddy attended Mass every day to thank God for their family and their health and to pray that we all would die in the state of God's grace. Everyone was expected to participate in the community life and service of the Church. She was a faithful member of the Altar Society, Catholic Women's Club and many fundraising committees for the Church. Committees weren't enough, as she personally paid to replace altar linens, vestments and, of course, to provide flowers for the altar.

During her years as a stay-at-home mom, she had interesting ways of bringing her point home to each of us. Often, when she got angry, she would pick up anything that was handy and throw it at whichever of the nine children was in her line of fire. She had great expressions, like, *"you don't smoke, because the Blessed Mother did not smoke,"* or when confused as to who she was reprimanding, she would recite all nine names, until finally she would say, *"you know who I am talking to."* Lessons were offered in strong, clear terms. If you repeated something she did not want anyone else to know, she would say that you *"are a damn liar"* if you did tell. But her quirks were completely overshadowed by her generosity to all. Stories are told and verified about all the extra mouths that were welcomed to the lunch and dinner table. *"With 11 already, what's one or two more?"* Often instead of two extra's, it was four or five. This was true on the annual Pawleys Island vacation when 11 became 13 with cousins Jan and Carol often in attendance for the week. One of the most poignant memories is when Mama and Daddy took in a struggling baby to help the young mother. They raised that child as one of us, until the child was a healthy infant and the family was in shape to take him back.

With her two oldest children in their late teens, she would take up her career as a business woman. Zion, in classic Joseph tradition, set up and successfully ran Colonial Florist on Front Street for a quarter of a century. It was here that much of Georgetown got a chance to interact with Mt. Zion. She was a good business woman, and no shrinking violet. She felt strongly about the local government, served on many a Board or Committee seeking to improve the quality of life in the community. She was never known to bite her tongue and had a great sense of right and wrong. This was clear as she attended many a City Council meeting to express her concerns.

The Mt. Zion appellation seemed appropriately fitting, as she combined her commitment to the Church with her belief in the rightness of her opinion. While operating Colonial Florist, Mama had put flowers on the altar each week and decorated the church for all occasions and Holy Days at no cost to the church. When it was time to decorate on the highest of Holy Days, Christmas and Easter, the intrepid Pastor announced his plan to choose volunteers to make decisions on those decorations. The dialog went something like this: Pastor, *"Zion, I am the head of the church, so we will do it my way!"* Mama's reply, *"You might be the head of the church but I am the neck of the church and the neck moves the head."* I guess it is obvious who won that argument.

There are so many stories that this vignette doesn't do it justice. Suffice it to say, Zion gave us more than money could buy: love, security, support, our faith and the knowledge of God's love. What more could any child ask from their mother.

VIGNETTE: DAVID THOMAS JOSEPH
"Love your God…love your family…and love your country…"
By Timothy Joseph, his son

David Thomas Joseph, son of Thomas and Barbara, was born in Georgetown, S.C. on May 8, 1925. He was the fifth child of seven. As with his three brothers and three sisters, he was born, not in a hospital, but in the family home. As is the story of most immigrants, his family came to America seeking greater economic opportunity and in search of religious freedom.

His Early Life
The early years of his life revolved around the family grocery store, his education, and the local Catholic Church. He was taught from a very early age that with success comes sacrifice. Each one of his siblings, along with his parents, helped run a successful local grocery store on Front Street in Georgetown. This small business was responsible for providing and educating this large family. The family was able to make ends meet. Although they had little from a monetary standpoint, the siblings would all agree, that they "longed for nothing."

A story that David and his family would often tell of their mother sums up what was truly important in their lives: a local customer would often come into the store bragging of her "riches." One day she came to the store wearing new diamonds on her hand and was quick to show Mom Joseph her new jewels. After showing them to Mrs. Joseph, she asked her, "Where are your diamonds?" She said without hesitation, "my diamonds are Johnny, Nimmer, Helen, Zion, David, Paul, and Pauline." No more needed to be said in that moment. David was formally educated in his early years in the local school system, although most of his "education" came by means of his family. The "rock" of this family that helped them endure the great challenges of their new lives in America was their Catholic faith. David was nicknamed "the bishop" by his brothers and sisters, and prayer was at the heart of this close family. A day did not go by without seeing their mother with a rosary in hand. This rosary was prayed upon so often and was so beloved that the strands of the rosary were linked together in many places by bobby pins. She would say often to her "diamonds," "the greatest gift I can pass onto you is the gift of your faith."

The Draft

In May of 1943, David turned eighteen years old. He, as all young men on their eighteenth birthdays, was drafted into the military to serve the United States in WWII. After training in Great Lakes, Michigan, he came home for a short visit; he was soon sent into military action serving as a medic for the Third Marine Division in the Pacific Theatre. He spent time on Iwo Jima and Guam. He was on active duty in the Pacific for close to two years. By the grace of God and the prayers of his family, his life was spared and he came home alive. He and his fellow surviving military veterans would always say, "The true heroes did not come home." These were defining years in his young life.

After the War

After returning home, David and his brother Paul were anxious to begin their college education. When trying to discern where they wanted to go to college, a local priest, Father Smelly, suggested Georgetown University. Their brother, Nimmer, who assumed the role as father figure after their dad's death, made a trip to Washington DC on behalf of his younger brothers. He met with the Dean of the College of Arts and Science, and expressed the need for more educated Catholics in South Carolina. In this state at this time, there were less than one percent Catholics; this part of the country was recognized by the church as a missionary area. What all transpired in that infamous meeting is not known, but what is known, is that they were both accepted! David went on to complete his undergraduate and dental school degree at Georgetown University with the help of the GI Bill.

Marriage

David was introduced to his future wife Rose Mary Sayeg by his cousin Marie Joseph. Marie and Rose Mary were classmates in Nursing School in Charleston, SC. She was of a Lebanese and Syrian heritage and this match was truly one "made in Heaven." Their love for one another was simply beautiful. They married in Miami, Florida, on July 4, 1951 and nine months to the day, April 4, 1952, their first daughter Jan Teresa was born.

New Dental Practice and Move to Camden, SC

In the summer of 1953, David and his young family moved to Camden, S.C., to start his new dental practice. A good friend of the family, Dr. Brockington, suggested to him that Camden was a nice town; DuPont was building a plant in the area and this town desperately needed a dentist with his Georgetown University education. In 1958, David welcomed his brother Paul into the Camden Dental practice. David and Rose Mary welcomed seven more children into their family. Not only was the dental office thriving, but so was the neighborhood. Next door, brother Paul and his wife Margaret also added eight children to their home; sixteen children were born between the two families in sixteen years!

Final Chapter

David went on to successfully practice dentistry for thirty-eight years. He and his wife humbly saw all of their children graduate from college and more. In 1991, David was diagnosed with pancreatic cancer. He faced this disease as he lived his life with passion, determination, and courage. He never said, "why me?" Instead, "thank you God for the many blessings you have bestowed on my life." He died surrounded by all of his family praying the rosary on April 18, 1992. He touched the lives of many by the example of the life he lived. He truly loved his God, and those who knew him saw it. He truly loved his family, and his family loved him for it. He loved his country, and his country was grateful for his service.

A Very Special Family

VIGNETTE: PAUL JOSEPH'S LEGACY
Lebanese Lakehouse

The pictures can't begin to capture it. This little vignette can't do it justice. You just had to be there. For years I had heard stories that the Camden branch of the Raad/Joseph clan had a hideaway on a lake. It took me 25 years in the family to get the secret map and a cherished invite.

Traveling two and half hours north from Georgetown on a beautiful sunny day, Mary Lou and I took a memorable Memorial weekend trek that eventually took us down a dirt road searching for a fork in the road that had a faux street sign: JOSEPH. We had arrived.

As the trees opened to a vista of grand Lake Wateree, we were confronted with dozens of cars spread across a huge back lawn. With the temperature hovering around 90, we thought we were in for a scorcher, only to be bathed in a strong soothing breeze off the lake. As we rounded the corner of the Joseph house, it was the sound that first hit me. It seemed like recess at school. Kids were everywhere. Cacophony ruled the day. There were kids on docks. Kids on boats. Kids playing ball on the lawn. Kids asleep in lawn chairs and deck chairs. Kids running in and out of houses. It was magical!

We were stopped at every turn by a friendly face, a welcoming hello and most often a hand or a hug. We knew none of the kids. They were third and maybe fourth generation Joseph family members and mostly from Camden, not Georgetown. Present today were second generation grandsons and granddaughters of the

John Kenny

first immigrant Raad/Joseph brother, Thomas and his wife Barbara. Thomas and Barbara had seven children: John, Nimmer, Helen, David, Paul, Zion and Pauline. This Memorial Day would have representatives of all seven, with the exception of Nimmer. Paul was the only first-generation member present, at age 89. At home in Georgetown, Paul's older sister, Helen, at 96, wasn't feeling up to the long ride. Imagine for a moment, six of Thomas and Barbara's seven children would have family members still close, still wanting to be together and still memorializing a family that grew from struggling immigrants who came to America over a century ago to build a better life for their family.

The day would unfold with introductions of me, the northerner and Irishman, to this mostly southern, Lebanese family. I say mostly, because over the years, the second and third generations had done what every melting pot American family had done; they married Greeks, and Italians, Germans and English and, yes, some were smart enough (!) to marry Irish. For me, there was no keeping track of who was who because you see, there were about 75 present this day who had come to celebrate Memorial Day and to revel in family, faith and fun. All were welcomed with open hearts and arms.

The Lakehouse was the brainchild of the inseparable, first generation, dentist brothers, David and Paul. For them, it was not good enough that each had had eight children, each built houses on abutting lots on Fair Street in Camden, and each practiced his profession in the same dental office. They bought a lake house "together" way back in 1948, according to surviving brother Paul: *I knew if we bought a beach house down in Pawleys Island, we wouldn't all be together. We would take turns and each family would take a week or two, but not be together. I knew, as the special sign on the wall still reads: IF WE BUILD IT, THEY WILL COME.* So Lebanese Lakehouse Lore was created, and a tradition of the family playing together was established – 70 years ago. The legacy continues!

This Memorial Day weekend felt like it added a bit of a coda on this family love story for the ages. It had been a difficult May. Early in the month, the family gathered to celebrate the passing of Paul's

A Very Special Family

sister, Pauline, at age 86. She was the youngest of the seven children of Thomas and his wife Barbara. Just weeks later, the family would gather in sadness again as Rosemary, brother David's wife passed away at age 88. Late on this Memorial Day, as the sun was beginning to head down across the Lake, ominous rain clouds formed as the entire family gathered on the grass. It was time for the traditional Catholic Sunday Mass to be said with the Lake as the backdrop. Father Bob Higgins would come all the way from Aiken to celebrate with the clan. He had been a family fixture for decades. Today's mass would be not only a celebration of America and of the Lord and our right to worship freely but also a celebration of two devoted Catholics, Pauline and Rosemary. The clouds threatened, but the rain held off. Father's sunny homily let us all imagine Pauline and Rosemary in heaven on each side of the Lord, scolding us for our sadness at their loss and urging us to carry on: pray, live, love.

As we left, Uncle Paul, the remaining scion of the clan approached Mary Lou and me, with a hug and tears in his eyes to thank us for coming. I was genuinely moved by his statement that our efforts to capture the history of this family brought great joy and happiness to him as he mourned the loss of his sister and sister-in-law.

We could not leave without Aunt Margaret entreating Mary Lou with raw Kibbeh for the long trip home. Faith and family and fun, and oh yes, in the finest Lebanese tradition, food, all ruled the day.

This, for me, will epitomize Memorial Day for the rest of my life.

THE JOSEPH FAMILY DENTAL DYNASTY
4 First Generation Josephs Become Dentists

We have talked a lot about the Joseph brothers and their entrepreneurial spirit. The first generation used their peddling skills and their love of good food and spirits to open a number of food-related businesses in Georgetown, Columbia and Beaufort, South Carolina. That first generation was intent on giving their children a leg up by letting them get an education and to become professionals. It would be the second generation that combined business, education and the medical profession to launch a Joseph family dental dynasty in the state of South Carolina that has created a true legacy in their field.

The four Joseph brothers came to South Carolina with little formal education from their home country of Lebanon. But they came with one of the signature traits/beliefs of so many immigrants: an abiding commitment that their children and grandchildren would have a better life and more opportunities than they had.

In their early days in their new country, the Catholic Church would play a critical role in helping the Lebanese immigrants to understand where their children would find those opportunities. As the first-generation Joseph children began to grow, the Church would steer them toward formal education as the ticket to success in the new world. First this was in Sunday school under Father James McElroy, Pastor of St. Mary's from 1931 to 1938. The family pictures in those early years show the Lebanese families in their Sunday-best attire at the various church school gatherings. A major contributor to their education effort was Father Richard Madden, who would go on to become a respected author and scholar. When he arrived in 1938, he and Father McElroy created St. Mary's elementary school. As recounted in a different chapter, St. Mary's Church and school would become the focal point of Lebanese family life in Georgetown. It provided education but so much more. It was entertainment, family gathering and the center of social activity.

Eventually it was the Catholic priests who would open to this first generation of Lebanese in South Carolina one of the finest universities in America; Georgetown, the city, would lead to Georgetown, the University. Father Madden had attended the College of Charleston and The Catholic University of America in Washington, D.C. He, along with the many other educated priests, who rode circuit throughout the Northeast, mid-Atlantic and South, would imbue in these young students a desire for higher education and the establishment of lofty business and professional goals. To listen to the Lebanese octogenarians I interviewed in 2013, it was the local Catholic clergy that first opened their eyes to these opportunities and then literally opened the University doors to them.

David Joseph had no plans to leave the state and had not considered applying to Georgetown University and its medical school. It was a St. Mary's parish priest who convinced him to consider, against tough odds, applying for admission. Nimmer traveled up to Washington and met with Georgetown University's Dean. Nimmer had to plead a tough case. His argument was simple: Georgetown University was formed in 1789 with the backdrop of rampant discrimination against Catholics. This discrimination would become deadly in the post-Civil War South, both against people of color and Catholics. At the time the Lebanese arrived in South Carolina, the Ku Klux Klan and the No Nothing Party were waging effective intimidation and violence campaigns. *(See separate chapter on the Lebanese race discrimination battles.)*

Nimmer argued that the heart of its mission was to serve these very immigrants and educate the future doctors and dentists that would return to serve their cities and towns throughout the South. The sales pitch was a success. As a result of that trip three sons of Lebanese immigrants would be accepted at Georgetown University – Paul, David and Arthur. Each would take his professional training back to his beloved South Carolina, and each would go on to serve families through the balance of the 20th century and into the 21st.

Amazingly, one-fifth of the first-generation Josephs would go on to become dentists (John, Paul, David and Arthur). A number of the second generation would do the same. It is truly an immigrant success story. Georgetown, Camden and Beaufort teeth have been lovingly cared for since Thomas Joseph's son John became a dentist in the 1940s.

From hindsight, it seems so fitting that these first and second generations would make such a mark in their communities as well as on the very University that three of them struggled to enter. In 1991, Georgetown University honored the Joseph dental dynasty by presenting Paul Joseph, on the occasion of his son Paul Jr.'s graduation from Dental School, the Georgetown University Parents Medal and plaque in recognition of their dedication to education and their commitment to the University.

Folklore, reported in *A Walk Down Front Street*, chronicling the history of the various merchants and businesses on Front Street in Georgetown through the 1900s, states that Dr. John Sr., upon returning from World War II, was pleased to open his dental practice at 701 Front Street on

> ### Georgetown University
> ### The Parents Medal
>
> This medal was established in 1982. Its purpose is to pay honor to all parents of the graduates of the College of Arts and Sciences who by their sacrifices and encouragement have helped their sons and daughters complete their studies in the College. It is awarded to representative parents who by their long and loyal association with Georgetown through these sons and daughters typify qualities of parenthood to be admired and respected. The medal shall be awarded at the discretion of the Dean of the College.
>
> ### The Joseph Family
>
> Paul Thomas Joseph, College '50 - Dental '56
> Ellen, Nursing '79
> Pauline, Nursing '81
> Paul, Jr., College '87
>
> Carium Joseph, College '50 - Medical '54   David Thomas Joseph, College '49 - Dental '53
> Margaret, Nursing '59   Timothy, College '90
> Kathleen, College '84
> Kevin, College '86
> Molly, College '88   Thomas Chester Joseph, College '66
>
> Honor your father and mother, as the Lord your God has commanded you, that you may live long and prosper in the land that the Lord your God has given you.

the second floor. This was said to be because he had lived there as a child when his parents lived above the N. Joseph & Brother General Store that his father Thomas operated with his brother Nicholas until the latter's death in 1920. I say "folklore" because of a luncheon conversation I had in 2013.

First generation siblings, Paul, Helen and Pauline (all children of Thomas), arranged a lunch for me at the River Room, inviting third generation cousins Johnny Joseph, Barbara Dumm, and Mary Lou Kenny. At the luncheon, I reiterated the story and Pauline added that she had been born at that same location on Front Street above the Nicholas & Brother's store. Pauline's older sister, then 92 but in great shape and with a strong memory, debunked that account as well as Pauline's home birth saga. When I pursued it further with Dr. John Joseph Jr., I learned that he had shared that account with the authors of *A Walk Down Front Street*, taking it on faith from his parents.

In any event the children and grandchildren of the four brothers have a hundred stories about their days in that set of buildings on Front Street where each of the brothers lived and ran businesses for 40 years. One of these buildings is also the home of Thomas Café (*see separate chapter*). Immigrant brother John Joseph had a son Alfred. He married Mary Louise Thomas. It was the Thomas family that opened and ran the Café for more than 50 years at that same location. As a result, Joseph's 701 and 703 Front Street locations are filled with more than a hundred years of Lebanese spirits and tales!

Dr. John Joseph, Jr, son of John Joseph, and Dr. Timothy Joseph, son of David Joseph, have continued the Georgetown dental practice set up in the 1940s by Dr. John Joseph, Sr. It is across the street from the original N. Joseph & Brother buildings at 701-703 Front Street.

Georgetown University would continue to be a major educational home to the second and third generation of Josephs. Over the course of 50 years literally dozens of direct descendants of the four Joseph brothers graduated from Georgetown University and went on to serve the people of South Carolina well.

A Very Special Family

The Camden Dental Story
Dr. David Joseph, DDS, Dr. Paul Joseph, DDS and Dr. Bobby Joseph, DDS

The Camden-based Joseph Dental Associates over half-century story is quite unique and exemplary of the Raad/Joseph history. Since 1953 Josephs have been offering quality dental care to families in Camden, S.C. Five of their employees have worked there for 45+ years, four have worked there for 25+ years.

Back in the 1950s a good friend and area orthodontist, Dr. Willie Brockington convinced Dr. David Joseph there was a great need for serving families with a general dentistry practice in Camden. The DuPont May Plant had recently started production in Lugoff and the general population was growing. So, in 1953, after graduating from Georgetown University Dental School, Dr. David T. Joseph, Sr. arrived in Camden with his wife Rosemary and their daughter Jan. Dr. David set up practice that summer renting space in the Pritchard Building behind the post office in downtown Camden. Dr. David joined dentists, Drs. Williford, Sowell and Hinson, already in Camden.

While Dr. David was establishing his practice, his brother Paul T. Joseph, Sr., was busy studying dentistry at Georgetown University Dental School. After graduating in 1956, Dr. Paul served two years with the Naval Dental Corp, assigned to the U.S. Marines at Parris Island, South Carolina. In 1958, Dr. Paul joined a very busy Dr. David. In the mid-1960s, Dr. Paul, along with the Kershaw County Dental Society and the Camden Jaycees, helped to fluoridate the public water supply. This low-cost public health service drastically reduced the occurrence of tooth decay in the county. The Doctors Joseph were also busy at home raising eight children *each*.

Dr. David's son Bobby joined the practice in the summer of 1990, after graduating from the Medical University of South Carolina School of Dentistry. Nine months later in February of 1991, sadly Dr. David was diagnosed with pancreatic cancer. He died April 22, 1992, after a courageous battle with the disease. *"Thank God I had those nine months to practice under his guidance before he became ill. I was able to witness first hand his caring ways and his philosophy of giving nothing but your best,"* Dr. Bobby shared. *"It was also a nice transition for our patients."* Dr. Paul's son, Paul Jr., joined the practice in the summer of 1992 after graduating from the Medical University of South Carolina School of Dentistry followed by a one-year general practice residency at Palmetto, Richland.

VIGNETTE: PAULINE JOSEPH SOTTILE
The Almost Nun and Her Immaculate Conception Twins

During one of the many videotaping sessions of the second-generation Josephs, we learned some charming backstories on the first generation.

Pauline Joseph Sottile was the youngest of the seven children born to immigrants Thomas Raad Joseph and Barbara Nahra Joseph. From multiple sources, it was clear that she was a very devoted Catholic from an early age and remained so throughout her 86 years of life. In the month after her death, in 2017, her two adult children, Vincent and Mary, along with her 90-year-old brother Paul delighted us with anecdotes, tales and even songs learned from Pauline, the inveterate school teacher. Two of my favorites are:

Mary told us that her mother went to mass practically every day of her life. In her early years in Georgetown, she would do this by riding her bike from home on Kaminski Street (where the International Paper Mill is now located) in the West End of Georgetown into the historic district to St. Mary's Church and then on to school. It was this early devotion that convinced Pauline that she wanted to become a Catholic nun. Apparently, one of the main reasons that this did not happen was due to the urging of her older brother Paul. As the story was being told by Mary, she reached over and held his arm and a big smile engulfed Paul's 90-year-old face: *"You told Momma that she couldn't be a nun, because you needed her to get married and have children so that her children and yours could grow up together, just as you had with brothers, sisters and cousins all around."* Well, the rest is history. Pauline's brothers had 22 kids and her sisters had 13 and the cousins seem too numerous to count. Paul's wish came true. For the rest of her life, Pauline would be surrounded by family and remain devoted to her faith.

We learned in this same interview, that Pauline's faith would intervene in another special way. Devotion to Mary, the mother of Jesus, is an integral part of Catholicism. One of the most important holy days in the Church is the Feast of the Immaculate Conception, celebrated on December 8 of each year. Although Pauline would not become a nun and she would not have 8 or 9 children like some of her siblings, she considered it a special blessing that her only children, twins, would be born on that very holy day. Of course, her daughter would be named in honor of the Blessed Virgin.

Pauline would remain close with her brothers, sisters, cousins and, of course, her children and very devoted to her faith and to Mary.

A Very Special Family

SHICKORY RAAD JOSEPH

Born in Lebaa, Lebanon (b. 1888 and died 1935)
Came to America at age 12 to be with his brothers:
    Nicholas, Thomas and John
Married to Sarah Frances (b. ? and died 1991)

They had 6 children:
    Ann Joseph
    Freda Joseph (in 2017, she is the eldest living Joseph
        descendant of the 4 brothers at age 100)
    Josephine Joseph
    Rose Joseph Keach
    Jeanette Joseph Gleaton
    Arthur Anthony Joseph

Shickory and Sarah had 12 grandchildren
    Ann's child:
        Patricia Joseph Ward

    Josephine's children:
        Philip M. Joseph, Jr.
        Donna Joseph Furlong
        John Michael Joseph

    Rose's children:
        Sherri Keach Jordan
        Eckerly Martin Keach, II
        Lee Mac Keach
        Mary Denise Keach Clements

Jeanette's children:
    Sarah Francis Gleaton Kirkland
    Janet Lynn Gleaton

Arthur's children:
    Arthur A. Joseph, Jr.
    Melanie A. Joseph

VIGNETTE: SHICKORY RAAD JOSEPH

Shickory Raad Joseph was the fourth and final brother to come to America. He did so when his brother Thomas traveled back from Georgetown to Lebaa to retrieve his sweetheart Barbara Nahra, who he had left behind in the old country when he traveled to America at age 15. While back on this trip, he and Barbara were married in the small Maronite rite Catholic Church in their village of Lebaa. When they decided to come back to America, the returning party was considerably larger for they brought with them brother Shickory and his wife Sarah Frances and young Thomas Elias Isaac.

The literal translation for the name Shickory in Arabic is "Thanks the Lord." As you will see from the story below, entreating the Lord and thanking the Lord was to be a major focus of Shickory and his wife Sarah.

Shickory and his wife's first five children were girls, Ann, Freda, Josephine, Rose and Jeanette. Freda and Josephine are still alive. Freda, as of the writing this chapter, is 99. Although Sarah loved her girls, like so many first generation immigrants from the old country, Shickory and Sarah wanted a boy. Apparently, Sarah was determined to have one. With Catholicism a major part of their lives, Sarah would seek the help of the Lord to bring her a son.

John Kenny

It was that son that I met with in Columbia in 2013. Dr. Arthur Joseph, in a wonderful, rambling conversation over a cigar and glass of wine, recounted his mother's entreaty to the Lord. According to Arthur, when he was quite young his mother told him of the deal that she had made with the Lord. If he would give her a son, she would make an annual pilgrimage to a tiny Catholic Church in Summerton, South Carolina, from their home in Beaufort. That church had been formed by another small group of Lebanese immigrants. They had come to America in 1899, one year before the first of the four Joseph brothers had come to Georgetown. For the first fifteen years, these Lebanese Catholics were being spiritually served by priests from St. Ann in Sumter some twenty miles away. Mass would be held in family homes. By 1914 the 10 men and 7 women, along with their 20 children, were able to build their own church in Summerton, St. Mary's.

Sarah delivered five daughters over a 12-year period in 1912, 1916, 1920, 1922 and 1924 (one daughter died in childbirth), praying all the time for a son, never giving up hope and never changing her deal with the Lord. Fifteen years would pass before Arthur was born in 1927. True to her word, beginning that year and continuing for the rest of her life, she would make an annual pilgrimage to the tiny St. Mary's Church to keep her side of the bargain.

Arthur was 86 when I interviewed him, and he proudly related that he has continued the pilgrimage and provided a very special addition to this wonderful story. He and his wife Dorothy had a son in 1958 and a grandson in 1992. The annual pilgrimage continues one hundred years later. Four generations have now carried it on into the 21st century.

In memory of his mother's devotion to God, Arthur wanted to have a memorial to his parents in the tiny church in Summerton. Unfortunately, all of the stained glass windows had been given in memory of the various Lebanese founding families and no space in the tiny church was apparently available. Arthur was not to be deterred. In 1978, fifty-one years after his birth, he approached the Catholic Bishop in Charleston and, after a great deal of negotiation, got permission to memorialize his parents. The decision was to knock out a massive piece of the back wall above and behind the altar to construct a stained glass window depiction of Lebanon's first Saint.

Saint Sharbel Makhluf was a Maronite monk, hermit and priest who had died in Lebanon one year before the first Lebanese families came to Summerton, South Carolina. It was Pope Paul VI who in 1977 canonized him and quoted Psalm 92:13, *"the just man shall flourish like the palm tree, like the Cedar of Lebanon."* The window is inscribed in memory of Arthur's parents, Mr. and Mrs. Shickory Joseph.

My wife and I made our pilgrimage to St. Mary's in 2014 as the current Bishop held a 100-year memorial mass one sunny Sunday. The church appeared little changed from how it was constructed in 1914. That day it was filled with ancestors of those Lebanese founders of the church and the small community of Summerton. On the windows were memorials to the Josephs and Isaacs and so many others, but in the pews were the proud, dedicated Lebanese descendants, especially Shickory and Sarah Joseph's only son Arthur, along with Arthur Jr. and William Arthur Joseph. Three generations prayed dutifully and had a chance to thank the Lord for Sarah's devotion, perseverance and her deal with the Lord to bring a son, a grandson and a great grandson into the world. The mass that day was a fitting coda to a wonderful drama played out over a hundred years.

VIGNETTE: DR. ARTHUR JOSEPH, DDS

In 2013, I had the wonderful opportunity to interview two of those first four Joseph sons who had gone on to become dentists: Paul and Arthur.

Arthur Joseph, son of Shickory, one of the last two brothers to arrive, at age 82 was retired and living in Columbia near two of his sisters, Freda, then 96, and Josephine, then 90. Unfortunately, the other first generation Joseph dentists (John Joseph Sr. and David Joseph) had passed away before I started this project. All of their stories of their path to dentistry were quite unique and interesting.

Arthur's introduction to Georgetown University Dental School is testimony to the power and influence of the first generation of immigrant children and how immigrant families helped each other. Arthur served in the U.S. Army in World War II, having only finished two years of high school at Winyah High in Georgetown. The military training and experience convinced him to pursue a career in mineral engineering. It was what interested him most. Upon returning home from the military, he applied for acceptance to the Colorado School of Mines, a venerable and unique

A Very Special Family

institution dating back to 1873. His military service trained him as a civil engineer. He liked the work, loved the challenge of engineering. But, a visit to Washington, D.C. to his cousins David and Paul would change all that. They were already dental students at Georgetown University. The trip was meant as a family visit and a chance to see the Nation's capital, but the brothers had different plans. They wanted to convince Arthur that the dental path would serve him better than minerals and mining and applied engineering. The problem was that Arthur had zero medical or dental training or schooling. Even more troubling was that he had not even finished high school. But these were different times in America and in U.S. education. There were no SATs, no cookie cutter applications. The country was rebuilding after a brutal war with Germany and Japan. The veterans that had saved the world for democracy and from tyranny had sacrificed immensely. Their education was in trenches and planes and ships, often in unimaginable circumstances that no college entrance exam could begin to test. So, Paul and David worked their magic charms on Arthur, convincing him to consider applying. Then Georgetown University had to be charmed.

Interviewing Paul in 2013 showed me that he still had that charm so many years later. Paul made the case to the President of Georgetown University that Arthur would be an asset to the school and later to the profession. If you have ever dealt with Jesuit Priests, you would know they are formidable in intellect and forensics. Paul charmed them. Arthur was given provisional acceptance, subject to returning to South Carolina to take a series of preliminary courses and score well. He obviously did so and became a major asset to Beaufort, South Carolina, where he decided to set up his dental practice for the next 40 years.

VIGNETTE: A CHURCH FORMS IN THE WILDERNESS

Summerton, S.C., in Clarendon County began to be populated in the 1830s. Plantation owners along the Santee River made their move inward to Summerton to escape from the mosquitos. According to Wikipedia: *It was thought of as a health resort and safe retreat from the "malaria" associated with the swamp. The town was officially chartered by the South Carolina legislative delegation on Christmas Eve, 1889.* [13]

Just as the town was being set up officially and at the same time as the Raad/Joseph brothers were arriving from Lebaa to Georgetown, S.C., a small group of Lebanese families, Josephs and Isaacs came to rural Summerton in the 1890s. The immigrants came to Summerton in search of employment and business opportunities. Like many areas in the South, there were no Catholics in Summerton and the closest Catholic Church was in Sumter, 20 miles away. The Catholic families would either make the journey to Sumter, or Catholic priests would come and celebrate mass in their homes.

By 1913, the Lebanese families came together and purchased a small parcel of land to build their own church in Summerton. In February of 1914, a small wooden chapel was built and named in honor of the Virgin Mary. St. Mary Catholic Church could accommodate 60 people and was visited regularly as a mission of St. Ann Catholic Church in Sumter. The church history states:

A Very Special Family

> *In April of 1917 Bishop William Russell blessed the church and recorded a total of 37 members of the congregation (10 men, 7 women and 20 children). The congregation in Summerton, the Catholic Register notes, is the only congregation in the diocese composed completely of Syrians (Lebanese).* [12]

St. Mary's would continue as a tiny church, even after the massive construction projects by the S.C. Public Service Authority in 1939 and 1941 resulted in Lake Marion and Moultrie and the Pinopolis hydroelectric plant and the dams on the new lakes. Eventually, a much larger church, Our Land of Hope, would be built in the growing city of Manning, but St. Mary's would survive.

My wife and I had the opportunity to attend the 100th anniversary in 2014. It was a wonderful Mass and festive luncheon with many 80- and 90-year-old representatives of the original Joseph and Isaac families in attendance. Possibly the proudest were the members of the Shickory Joseph family whose mother had promised an annual pilgrimage to St. Mary's, if God would bless her with a son to complete her family of five girls. Dr. Arthur Joseph attended and was able to recount all of his mother's pledge and to point to the stunning stained glass window of St. Sharbel over the altar that his family erected in memory of his mother.

The commemorative brochure handed out on the 100th anniversary seemed to provide a perfect example to how 37 immigrants at the turn of the 20th century would build a church for the ages and a legacy of love:

> *The history of St. Mary Church is not complete without the mention of the St. Mary/Our Land of Hope food pantry. The food pantry was started in 1991 and operates from a refurbished house next to St. Mary church building. The food pantry regularly serves more than 300 needy families each month from the area through the volunteer efforts. This effort represents the answer of the parishioners of St. Mary/Our Lady of Hope to the call of Christ in the Gospel, when he challenged his disciples to give the people something to eat, rather than send them away. (Mt. 14:16)* [12]

JOHN RAAD JOSEPH

Born in Lebaa, Lebanon (b. 1890 and died 1963)
Came to America at age 14 to be with his brothers:
    Nicholas, Thomas and Shickory
Married to Selma Azouri (b. ? and died 1963)

They had 4 children:
    Amelia Joseph Isaac
    Nellie Joseph Dorian
    Alfred Paul Joseph, Sr.
    Marie Joseph Franks

John and Selma would go on to have 10 grandchildren
    Amelia's children:
        Linda Isaac Miller
        Joseph Isaac Jr.
        Martha Ann Isaac

Nellie's child:
Selma Dorian Davis

A Very Special Family

Alfred's children:
    Mary Louise Joseph Kenny (author's wife)
    Sandra Joseph Cornelius
    Tina Joseph Hatchell
    Alfred Paul Joseph, Jr.

Marie's children:
    John Franks
    Robert Franks

VIGNETTE: JOHN RAAD JOSEPH
(My Wife's Grandfather)

John Raad Joseph was born in Lebaa, Lebanon in 1890. He was the youngest of six children with three brothers and two sisters. His two sisters Helen and Saada never emigrated to America. It was John's oldest brother Nicholas who was the first of the Raad family to leave the old country for a better life in America. He did so in 1900. Within four years, he encouraged two of his remaining brothers, Thomas and John, to join him in Georgetown. Thomas came to Georgetown with his brother Shickory and wife Sarah Frances and their young cousin, Thomas Elias Isaac. Each of the brothers had left parents and siblings and ventured to a new, unknown world.

John was by all accounts of those I interviewed, "the smallest and the most loved." He was a quiet and shy man who just went about his business "always lost in the crowd." In an interview with Victoria Joseph, she opined that early on, Georgetown must have seemed crowded with the various Lebanese from the tiny village of Lebaa who had emigrated to this seaport town, because John left Georgetown not too long after he arrived. Another Lebanese family, the Azouris had begun their new life in a nearby town in South Carolina. On a peddling trip, John found and wooed Selma Azouri, who later became his bride. They decided to try their fortunes elsewhere. For nine years, John and Selma operated a restaurant in Columbia, South Carolina. They moved for a time to Hopewell, Virginia and eventually returned to South Carolina, initially settling in

A Very Special Family

Hemingway. Sometime around 1915, they came back to Georgetown, where they would stay the rest of their lives, raising their four children, Amelia, Nellie, Alfred and Marie.

In keeping with the Joseph/Lebanese tradition, when they returned they set up shop in the food business, a meat market. This would be the first of many such businesses that John and Selma would own and run over the next fifty years. During this time, they ran butcher, fruit and vegetable, liquor and dry goods stores. They all had one thing in common, they were family owned and operated, with all in the family lending a hand. According to those I interviewed, "John made and lost several fortunes." This was not because he was unsuccessful in business, but rather because he had an outsized heart. He lent money to many, gave away food and goods and more, and could not turn away a needy family. He was generous to a fault. Everyone could count on him for both a hand stretched out and the proverbial handout. Many of these businesses were set up and run through the Great Depression, which took a brutal toll on Georgetown, like much of the country. As my wife tells it, "Even when they knew the family, black or white, was unable to pay for their goods, they gave them what they needed. They never wanted a child to go hungry." The legacy of this sharing was front and center when their grandson ran for City Council in 2015. As his mother in a wheelchair, accompanied by his sister Mary Lou, campaigned throughout the city, families who had been the beneficiaries of those friendships came forward to share their stories. Louise and Mary Lou Joseph would be recognized immediately, and love and support was offered.

Initially, like so many other immigrants, John and Selma and their children lived in rental housing on Pennsylvania Avenue, paying weekly rent and working hard to make ends meet. John was the brother who would give you the shirt off his back, and often did. It was John who was chosen by his three brothers to travel back to Lebanon to sort out the family property and businesses. Some say, he was too generous to those who remained in Lebanon as properties were sold or given away. I learned in an interview with Dolly Raad Akwah (who is the subject of a later chapter), that while John was in Lebaa settling the family property, he was asked by her parents to serve as her Godfather, thus tying the old country with the new.

Eventually, things got better and John and Selma bought a house on Highmarket Street in Georgetown, just steps away from their meat market. It became the focal point for the extended family Sunday dinners, holiday celebrations and the many other occasions to enjoy sumptuous, savory Lebanese cuisine. Selma was a fabulous cook and, by many accounts, the best in the family. Everyone was welcome at these all-day Sunday affairs. Food and drink establishments would be the staple of John and Selma's business life, but family would be their passion.

As is true in most first-generation immigrants, it was those male heirs that were doted on. My wife shares the following about her grandfather and her only male sibling:

> *John, like most, wanted a grandson to carry on the family name. He and Selma had three daughters and one son, Alfred. So, it fell to Alfred and his wife Louise to grant him that wish. It didn't happen for a very long time. Alfred and Louise had three girls who John loved very much, but he still wanted the grandson. As was the case in the first half of the 20th century, many children were lost in delivery. Louise was no exception, but Louise was a determined woman. She had lost two babies. At 41 she gave birth to that son, Alfred Paul, Jr. – ten years younger than her youngest daughter, and seventeen years younger than her oldest one. John was ecstatic. In the old Lebanese tradition, John went out back and shot his revolver to signify the birth of a grandson. The entire family had prayed for this child for many years and on the way home from the hospital, the entire entourage stopped at St. Mary's to introduce the child to the church and to thank the Blessed Mother to whom they'd prayed for years and who they believed intervened to grant their wish. The doting would continue. Every day on John's way to and from work, he stopped by Alfred's house to see his grandson. He would walk in, go upstairs where the baby was in his crib or into the family room and just stand over the crib staring at the child and thanking the Lord for this great gift. Some days the rest of the family didn't even see John during his visit. Each day, after school, one of the two older sisters had to put Alfred in the stroller and walk him downtown to be seen by his grandfather.* [31]

John may have had a premonition about what he was doing and why he spent so much time with his only grandson. John died unexpectedly of a heart attack when his grandson was only two years old. He died happy with the knowledge that he had "an heir and a spare."

John and Selma made quite a couple and, like many successful spouses, they were opposite in many ways. John was quiet and shy. Selma was a big woman with a big personality and was a world class story teller. She spoke in broken English and had the most contagious laugh you ever heard. She would tell stories in a combination of Arabic and English about her four children and tears would stream down her face as she laughed and cried all at once. Even when one could not understand what she was saying because of the laughter and broken English, you were swept into the story and the fun. She could entertain an entire room and leave them all in stitches. She could make the most boring or scariest event the funniest thing you ever heard.

Immigrant parents were simultaneously protective of their children and also willing to assert their discipline. John and Selma were no different. On the discipline side, like in so many homes, son Alfred would be mischievous and the oft heard expression *wait until your father gets home* would be threatened. In the meantime, Selma told how she couldn't catch young Alfred so would throw her shoes at him in a vain attempt to make her point. Eventually John would arrive home, grab the razor strop, and tell Alfred to hold onto the brass bed and take his punishment. Of course, by the time Alfred was a teenager, he towered over his father and could have easily stopped the punishment, but he, like all of the siblings, loved and respected his father and would never challenge him. While all of this sounds horrible in today's American society where we are so averse to any form of corporal punishment, it was hysterical when told by Granny Selma!

Ever on the protective side, Selma did not want son Alfred to play football because she was afraid he would get hurt. But he was a natural athlete, and his friends and coaches and others in town apparently streamed into the Joseph store "begging" her to let him play. She relented and, as you will see, it was a wise choice because Alfred would become a star athlete in three sports.

VIGNETTE: AMELIA AGNES JOSEPH ISAAC
Family, Faith and Food
By Linda Miller, Joe Isaac and Martha Ann Isaac, her children

Amelia Agnes Joseph was the first-born child of John and Selma Azouri Joseph. She was born in Georgetown in 1915, 11 years after her father had emigrated from Lebanon. She would be joined in the family by two sisters, Nellie and Marie and her brother, Alfred.

Because of the Depression, Amelia began work at the age of 13 to help support her family. She recalls caring neighbors, who could never admit publicly they were friends with "the foreigners," leaving baskets of groceries on their front porch. She often said that without the kindness of the townspeople, they would have starved. Amelia was a straight A student and went to work at the Georgetown County Department of Social Services upon her graduation from Winyah High School.

Amelia fell in love with another member of the Georgetown Lebanese community, Joseph Isaac. They married on 23 July 1943 at St. Mary Church in Georgetown after Joe had left The Citadel to join the United States Navy. Amelia traveled with him to New York, California, Maine and Maryland, but returned to Georgetown when Joe was deployed in the Pacific. They lived with Amelia's parents after Joe returned from the service (early 1946 through mid-1947) while building a house at 1212 Prince Street where they reared their three children, passing on their love of family, faith and food.

Joe recalls a childhood of hardship, often describing his misery in cutting and bringing in wood for the stove and fireplace. Their experiences, though different, created an imperative to ensure the lives of their children were enriched with experiences and schooling that was not afforded them due to the circumstances of the times.

They grew up as part of a Lebanese clan who were determined to rear apple pie American children. This first generation recognized early that education was the true path to assimilation, but they remained fiercely loyal to their heritage, its cuisine and their Catholic faith. Joe and Amelia and their peers lived in two worlds: the Lebanese home with its attendant religious, cultural and language demands; and the world of 20th century Georgetown, S.C., where there was little understanding of non-European immigrants and their cultural norms and a healthy skepticism about Catholics and Catholicism. It was through their intellect, schooling, athletic prowess, and their ability to make friends wherever they were that they began to build the personal and professional respect and admiration that were hallmarks for both Joe and Amelia as their lives progressed.

Joe was devoted to extended family and was deeply religious. Because he had a key to the church, he would visit any hour of the day and night. Hardly a Sunday passed that the family was not visiting someone. Joe piled the family into the car and off we went to our grandparents or relatives in Charleston, Greeleyville, Kingstree, Great Falls or Mooresville.

Amelia was revered for her culinary prowess. There was never a week where some Lebanese dish did not appear on the table – hummus, kibbe, chicken and rice, stuffed squash, rolled cabbage and other more exotic preparations were on regular rotation. We shared many meals with the family of Alfred Joseph. When Amelia and Louise Thomas Joseph joined to put a meal on the table, they bested the finest restaurants. Before Easter and Christmas every year, Amelia and Louise spent hours together baking sambusak, aras, mahmoul and baklava. Their combined skills produced pastries that were worthy of James Beard acclaim.

At both Thanksgiving and Christmas, the family gathered in the early days around the table set by Amelia's parents, John and Selma to enjoy a feast of traditional American holiday foods as well as a host of Lebanese classics. Later, this was taken over by their daughter, Nellie. They were joint cultural celebrations in every way.

On the Feast of the Epiphany, the day in the Lebanese tradition when little Christmas is celebrated, the family gathered to have Z'leby, the Lebanese version of fried dough. We gathered most often at the home of Alfred and Louise Joseph to maintain this cultural tradition. Louise fried pan after pan of the treat and provided lots of syrup for dipping. Amelia was her kitchen partner, but it was Louise who kept the tradition alive for the family.

Amelia's career post-WWII was spent at the Department of Education. She had the title of "Clerk," which translated to Accountant for the Georgetown County Department of Education. During her tenure she created a new accounting system for the Department which came to the attention of the South Carolina Department of Education. That Department was so impressed with the methodology she developed, they asked Amelia to present her system to a symposium for other South Carolina school accounting personnel.

For many years, the front office of the Georgetown County Department of Education was over-represented by women of Lebanese heritage. Amelia Joseph Isaac handled the accounting, Mabel Isaac Walker was the administrative assistant to the Superintendent of Education, and Louise Thomas Joseph was administrative assistant to the Department's Manager of Business Operations. These women not only shared a common ethnic and religious heritage, but were professional colleagues as well.

Joe and Amelia were both active socially. Joe was a leader of the Knights of Columbus, the Moose Lodge and the VFW. In addition, he coached girls' softball in the Church League and pitched for the St. Mary Church men's softball team. Amelia was part of the Catholic Women's Club and played bridge with a group of women from the church for more than 30 years. They were called Le Jeudi Huit – The Thursday Eight.

Joe and Amelia never left a doubt that their children were loved unconditionally. They were determined to support us whatever path we chose and to ensure we never suffered for our faith or heritage. Joe and Amelia shared a passion for maintaining and nurturing their relationships with their children.

Wherever their children lived, they visited on a regular basis. When Linda moved to Maryland in the late '60s, Joe and Amelia visited several times a year. Martha Ann recalls Joe coming home from work on any given Friday, saying pack your bags, and off they went for another visit to Maryland. When Martha Ann and a cousin moved into an apartment in Atlanta, Joe arrived on the doorstep before it could be completely furnished. When he realized there was no dining table, he complained that a table and chairs were needed in order to eat meals together. They immediately piled into his station wagon and went to a flea market outside of Atlanta. That night they sat together as a family around the new dinette set and had one of Joe's favorite meals: eggs, bacon, grits and biscuits. Joe, Jr., an outstanding Citadel Hall of Fame football player, played few games without his parents there to cheer him on with a tremendous sense of pride.

Joe, Jr. experienced Joe and Amelia's determination to ensure their children were never punished for the practice of their faith. Joe and two other Catholic players were suspended from the basketball team for a game because they missed school to go to church. Joe, Sr. in no uncertain terms, informed the school administration that he would not stand for such discrimination. The suspension was lifted.

Joe, Sr. went to church every day. On Saturday he would go to 7:00 a.m. Mass at the Morgan House, often informing Joe, Jr. that he was coming, too, as Father needed a server. Joe, Jr. had the privilege of being the first person to whom Joe, Sr. gave Holy Communion upon his becoming an Extraordinary Minister of the Holy Eucharist. Joe, Sr. was brought to tears and Joe, Jr. was overwhelmed to be the first recipient and to recognize his father's deep love of God.

Joe and Amelia loved people and they were loved in return. Their intellect and personalities won over people who had never interacted or socialized with Lebanese Catholics. People truly "forgot" that they were Catholic or Lebanese. They were just good people who cared about their community and the people in it. Joe and Amelia modeled behavior that left their children with a commitment to stand up for what is right, whether it be related to family, profession, or others being unfairly maligned. They expressed unconditional love and never demanded more than they gave. They were a special couple who weathered cultural and personal storms to emerge as respected citizens who cared for family, community and country. God bless them.

Family, faith and food. These words define the priorities of Amelia and Joseph Isaac, but Joe and Amelia gave a depth of meaning to those words that prompt their children to say, "we had the best parents ever." Joe and Amelia put those three words into action through their unconditional love of their children, their commitment to visiting and remaining friends with extended family, their devotion to Catholicism and St. Mary Church, and Amelia's superb culinary skills.

VIGNETTE: NELLIE JOSEPH DORION
An Author in the Family

One of the more memorable characters in the Lebanese community in Georgetown was the powerful first-generation woman, Virginia (Nellie) Joseph Dorion. She was my wife's aunt on her father's side. She was born in the State of Virginia. Both of her parents were born in Lebanon in the 1890s. Everyone knew her as Nellie. I always thought of Nellie as smart as a whip, opinionated, outspoken. It was she who first shared the truism about her family with me: "We may speak Arabic, but we are Phoenicians." The phrase was never offered as a casual remark, but as a correction to a possible misinterpretation. She needed the listener to understand the depth of this family, its rich history, its roots. Her mother's family had a long heritage as professionals, while her father's family were farmers. Both were teenagers when they arrived in this new country by steamship through Ellis Island. Neither could speak English, but each would become merchants and business owners.

So, it was noteworthy that this Joseph woman became the first published author in the family. Nellie married, and she and her husband adopted a little girl. She needed the world to know her story, the family story of the Lebanese immigrants in Georgetown. In 1994, *Nellie My Story* was published by Nellie J. Dorion [21]. The book jacket offers an interesting commentary:

> *Life was not easy for Mrs. Dorion during her early years, which included the experience of the Great Depression of the early 1930s. Yet the author overcame the odds, and through determination, hard work and "maybe some luck,"… helped her family through.*

Nellie's story is succinct, but filled with amazing anecdotes that make you wish you knew this family… no, let me rephrase that, make you wish you *were* this family. Here are just a few.

In her younger years, she, her brother, two sisters and parents lived above the grocery store that their parents ran:

Those were good years when we lived on the corner of Highmarket and St. James. There were a lot of children in the neighborhood to play with. We kept the sidewalks hot with our roller skates.

The reader can almost feel and taste the excitement of that childhood.

My brother (Alfred) had a little red wagon and a Billy goat. He would hitch the goat to the wagon and we would take a ride. I remember the day the goat died. We missed him one day and started looking for him. We found him in the storeroom behind our store leaning against the wall in a corner, with his eyes wide open, dead. We were shocked beyond belief. I saw that goat in my dreams long afterwards.

Nellie offers us a glimpse into the immigrant businesses of her youth.

After we moved from the corner store (my father was looking for a better location) he opened a fruit stand on Front Street diagonally across from Fogel's Department Store. He brought a truck and hauled his fruit from Florida, mostly oranges, grapefruit, and bananas by the bunch, and he hauled peaches from McBee, S.C. Occasionally, he would let one of us ride in the truck with him to pick up his load of fruit. We loved it.

Those turned out to be the halcyon days for the family. The Great Depression hit Georgetown with a vengeance and the immigrants felt the brunt of it.

My father lost everything, including what little savings he had in the local bank. We had to move where the rent was cheap – a block of green shingled row houses, all alike, located at the end of town. The rent was five dollars a month... There were times when my father didn't even have the five dollars to give him and he would threaten eviction. Money was awfully scarce. Food was scarce. Our weekly baths were in a galvanized tub in the kitchen which was heated by a wood stove. Of course, we had a standard bathroom but we couldn't use the tub because there was no hot running water. Things were really tough.

A Very Special Family

Despite the hardship, Nellie ends her discussion of the era with this upbeat note:

Even though we didn't have anything to speak of, materially, those years were the most fun times of my life. I suppose being a very young person had much to do with it. They are the warmest in my memory.

Remember that the Depression era was also the Prohibition era. It didn't stop the consumption of alcohol, it just made it illegal and more expensive. To hear the 80- and 90-year-olds that I interviewed, alcohol was everywhere, as was gambling. It was the nature of America in the 1920s and 1930s. Nellie puts a pro-family and pro-business spin on it:

My brother Alfred also contributed monetarily by working at odd jobs. He was still going to school. There was one job in particular he didn't like – hauling moonshine for several businessmen. He was always afraid he would get caught because he knew it was against the law.

As it turned out, he did get caught. When the policeman brought him home to his father, there was hell to pay. No formal charges, but clear, concise justice at home. He learned his lesson well and became a model citizen.

Nellie explained how God and religion played a major role in the lives of these immigrant families:

My father and mother were very religious. They tried to instill love of God, Country and Church in us. I remember my father making us kneel around the dining room table every night, supported by the chairs, to say the entire rosary, plus several other prayers to the Blessed Virgin Mary.

But Nellie's story as a whole book is a cathartic statement of the child of an immigrant who lived dirt poor at times but never felt in need. It is about a kid growing up on happy city streets enveloped by the store fronts of dozens of Lebanese merchants who had come to America to find and build better lives. These are stories of living above those stores, or in tenements at 5 dollars a month with few amenities, but of being rich in so many ways.

VIGNETTE: NELLIE JOSEPH DORION
Author, Artist, Mama
By Selma Dorion Davis, her daughter

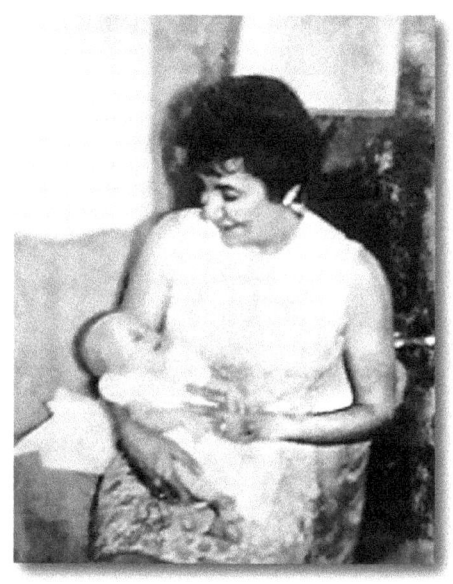

I think about my mother so often, but it's not often that I am asked to reflect on the 41 years we spent together and write about it. It is difficult to narrow a lifetime of experiences into a few paragraphs that simultaneously tell her story and honor her life.

It is possible that my mother was prophetic. Before Alzheimer's took her memories of an incredible life, she wrote it all down with the flair and flourish only Nellie could pull off and provided me, her only child, with a written account of her life and the family she so dearly loved.

She started writing that book when I left for college in 1986 and kept it a secret from me. I came home one holiday and stumbled across her manuscript which was written in longhand on a yellow legal notepad. She typed the entire book on a manual typewriter that she no doubt bought 40 years before, and used carbon paper so she would have two copies. I never told her that I found those drafts. When she finally told me that a publisher picked up her story and said they would print it, she beamed with pride. Photographers came to take her picture for the book jacket and the *Georgetown Times* wrote an amazing article about my mother, an author and local celebrity. She achieved this "fame" much later in life, but I am fairly certain that, when she was a child, she told herself she would write a book one day and that's exactly what she did. Books were like gold to her.

In addition to being an author, my mother was an artist. Just as she waited until I was away at college to write her book, she began painting with reckless abandon at the same time. She loved to take her little Kodak camera, with the square flash bulbs that turned a quarter turn with each snap, to locations that spoke to her: Pawleys Island, downtown Georgetown, and her backyard, all of which became the subjects of her paintings. She even painted a portrait of me from a photograph. My son, Henry, the grandson she held once, says it's definitely his favorite. My house is filled with her works, some signed Nellie J from the time she painted before I was born, and most with her initials NJD, the later years.

The nexus of my home and the homes of my aunts and uncles was the kitchen, specifically the kitchen table. That's where real life happened. So many of my friends remind me of the meals they ate at her little table in the sunny yellow kitchen. Mama was the best cook. Consistency was the key. Her rolled cabbage looked and tasted the same each time. It was another work of art with heaven-sent flavor.

Visiting was something we did regularly, and I learned to listen and soak up all the stories from her friends and family. As a small child I spent much of my time with the older generation and ate Lebanese delicacies all over town!

Mama was a consummate student. She loved learning about all sorts of subjects and, moreover, loved debating the finer points of her knowledge. All of my cousins will attest to this, but the raucous debates she would have with my cousin, Ken Miller, were her favorites, and I now know they were his favorites as well.

For so many years it was just me and Mama, a widow in 1970 raising an adopted girl on her own. My mother was a hard-working woman. She worked at The Mill and came home every day smelling like she worked in the mill rather than as the secretary to the president. Her strength was unflappable on the outside but inside, she was a very tender-hearted woman who sacrificed much so that her daughter could have every opportunity possible. She never sacrificed taking me to church, and we would go to Mass on Saturday evenings, head over to Hardee's for two roast beef sandwiches and rush home to eat on TV tables in the den while we watched Lawrence Welk and the Disney movie.

At the time I didn't know the gem that I had for a mother and I miss her terribly. I am who I am today because of her. I love deeply, cook madly, and have a thirst for learning and adventure that's unquenchable. Thank you, Mama.

VIGNETTE: MARIE JOSEPH FRANKS

Marie Joseph, born on March 25, 1925, was the youngest of John and Selma's four children. She was the only one of their children who lived away from South Carolina the majority of her adult life.

Marie graduated from Winyah High School and like many of the Joseph women left for Charleston and St. Francis School of Nursing where she earned her RN certification. While in Charleston, Marie met the man she would marry, Bob Franks, a WWII veteran who was studying at The Citadel. Bob and Marie moved to East Orange, N.J. to begin their new life. Marie had a difficult pregnancy that left her unable to have children. She and Bob adopted two boys, John Andrew and Robert Alfred, and she became a stay-at-home mom. As her son Bob describes it, *"she enjoyed raising her two boys in a world that resembled the well-known TV sitcom Leave It To Beaver."*

When her sons, John and Bob went off to school, Marie enrolled in Union County College in Cranford, N.J. and earned her degree. After fifteen years away from her profession, Marie restarted her nursing career. While she loved staying home raising her children, she was thrilled to be back in the hospital taking care of patients. In each of her positions in nursing, she was revered as a caring, knowledgeable and assertive professional who gave and demanded excellent care for her patients

Bob's engineering career took them to Ft. Washington near Oxon Hill, Maryland, where he was one of the original designers of the Washington, D.C. subway system. Marie worked during that time at Southern Maryland Hospital Center. Marie and Bob moved to Colts Neck, N.J. from which Bob rode the train every day to his job in New York City. After a few years, Bob and Marie returned to Maryland, this time living in Bowie. Bob commuted to a job in Washington, D.C., and Marie became a valued nurse at Anne Arundel Medical Center in Annapolis.

Despite her separation from South Carolina, Marie managed to stay in touch with family that was nearby. During her time in Cranford, she regularly issued invitations to her nieces and cousin who lived in the Northeast to spend the weekend with the Franks' family. Those weekends live large in memory as times of good food, laughter and a heavy dose of Marie's philosophy of life which she loved to espouse to her young family members. During both of her sojourns in Maryland. Marie regularly visited with her nieces who lived nearby, ensuring that many weekends and holidays were spent with family.

Marie never wanted to lose contact with Georgetown and her family there. Every year, twice a year, she packed her family in the car and they drove to Georgetown. The Franks family was always central to the Christmas celebration at Marie's mother's house who adored having her two grandchildren in her house if only briefly. In the summer, the Franks' stayed for two weeks at Pawleys Island, and during that time Marie made it a point to visit with immediate family and her many cousins who lived there. Marie's commitment to family ensured her children a connection to her childhood home and a relationship with their cousins.

She and Bob built a house in Hagley Estates in Georgetown County and moved there to be close to the family. Unfortunately, shortly before moving there, Marie was diagnosed with incurable cancer and died at the age of 57. She was the youngest of John and Selma's children but the first to die. She loved being home and spending her final three years with her family and childhood friends.

VIGNETTE: ALFRED PAUL JOSEPH, SR.
(My Wife's Dad)

Many parts of this work were difficult for me to write, mostly because I had never undertaken such a project before. This section is hard to write, because it is so emotional for me. Alfred is a legend. He was what others wish they could be. There are tears rolling down my cheeks as I write this. Capturing what causes that is daunting. If you were fortunate enough to have known him, you do not need it to be explained. He just was Alfred. Alfred died, twelve years to the day that I wrote this section. He died on that most horrendous day in America in my lifetime, 9-11-01. At his funeral mass, the Catholic priest, who had only known him for a short time captured Alfred's essence well:

> *I believe that the outpouring of love and support shown toward him and his family by your presence today would humble Alfred. I believe that he would say these or similar words: Why is everyone making such a big fuss over me? I haven't done anything special. I was only doing what I should be doing and that is to try my best to give the love that God has given to me and share that love to those around me.* [1]

He was a humble man, a gentle man, a God-fearing man, who stood large, loved deep and left a lasting impact on those he touched.

Alfred was born on October 9, 1918, the third of four children. He was the only son. He had inherited from his father his personality, charm and charisma. They were both shy and quiet men. This was the year that Germany had collapsed and the so-called "Great War," World War I, ended.

340,000 Americans had died during that war and another 675,000 Americans had died as a result of the 1918-1919 influenza pandemic. Alfred's father, John, was older than the mandatory age to be drafted and had not been conscripted. Alfred's first ten years of life was one of the more stable periods in America of the next fifty years. By the time he was 11, the U.S. stock market had crashed setting off the Great Economic Depression, and ten years after that, America and the world would be dragged into the Second World War. According to the history books, America became the wealthiest nation in the world with no obvious rivals during Alfred's formative years, the so-called "roaring 20s." They were interesting days in Georgetown, and sports ruled the day.

Football

Being a business owner as new immigrants was a ticket into acceptance in America and the South and Georgetown. The ticket for many in the first generation born to those immigrants was sports. America has always loved its sports, but the South has crazy love for sports and its athletes. As I wrote this chapter in 2013, America was literally "a twitter" about Heisman trophy recipient Johnny "Football" Manziel, the quarterback of the Texas A&M college football team. In 1935 and 1936, here in Georgetown, it was Alfred and the Georgetown "Big Train" Winyah Gators high school football team that everyone was excited about.

Eighty years later as I wrote this, I did not have to go far to ask who was Georgetown's best football player in the 1930s, for those who saw him play, they say he was Georgetown's best ever. It was Alfred. He is a sports legend in town eight decades after he last touched a football.

U.S. Army Brigadier General (Ret.) Lewis E. Maness published a reminiscence book in 2000 about his career called: *QB to BG, Quarterback to Brig. General*. In it, this World War II general takes us back to his senior year at Winyah High in Georgetown in 1936 with all of the drama and hoopla that high school sports in the South epitomizes. He recounts epoch rivalry games against the high schools in Andrews and Camden. The drama in his book and the newspaper stories of the time is palpable. It is he who forever puts Alfred, the athlete, in simple context. The team that year was full of the first-generation Lebanese immigrants. There were Isaacs, and Asseys and the ever-present Josephs:

> *In 1936, my Senior year at Winyah High, our football team had earned a reputation as a fast, hard hitting team that would score a lot of points. We had won five straight games when we went over to play Andrews High School in Andrews. We had such players as… Alfred Joseph, at fullback, (probably the best athlete in the state)…* [33, p22]

The *Georgetown Times* news story recounting the final game of the year against Camden, reads like something out of a recently aired book and TV series, *Friday Night Lights: A Town, A Team, and A Dream* by H.G. Bissinger. Georgetown lost the big game on a foul call after scoring the winning touchdown with no time remaining. That night captured the essence of Alfred perfectly. He was the epitome of an American football legend: *Big Alfred Joseph broke through and blocked Camden's kick and we recovered it on the thirty-yard line*. The team went on to score and believed they had won the game. But it was his brother-in-law Pete Thomas, who at age 89, in 2013 captured the rest of the story and gave a sense of what made Alfred great. Everyone in town was at the game and everyone was outraged at the bad foul call and the loss. Pete remembers walking home an hour after the game and finding Alfred on the front steps of his home, weeping. Here was the 6 foot 1 inch best athlete in the state, the big fullback, unabashedly in tears over a loss that affected him and his entire town. Alfred that day was at his finest, at once the powerful athlete and the caring soul.

This book is about the Lebanese and their storybook families. Alfred's portion of that reads like an episode out of *Tom Sawyer*. Alfred's daily routine exemplified how first-generation life in a small town was lived. After working a tough 10 or more hours at the International Paper Mill, Alfred would always help out at closing time at one of the Lebanese merchants' stores. It could be his dad's meat market or any one of the dozen different Lebanese markets along Front or Highmarket or

Church streets. To this family, work was the rule, not the exception. Just as Alfred's wife, Louise, would rush from her full-time job at the Department of Education to help serve lunch at Thomas Café, Alfred would clean aisles, stock shelves or man the register.

The family stories turn more interesting when they slide over to some of those "other" businesses that were run in the roaring 20s. Prohibition, a national ban on the sale, production and transportation of alcohol was in place in America from 1919 to 1933. The law could not stop people's desire for alcohol, so the production, sale and transportation continued. The Lebanese merchants of Georgetown owned and operated liquor stores before and after prohibition. This meant that during those 24 years, their role in the sale or transportation of alcohol was limited to "moonshine."

Former Georgetown attorney, Tom Rubillo, wrote a detailed article about prohibition in Georgetown that was published in the *Georgetown Times* on October 9, 2012. He offers the following overview, leading with the wonderful quote from a New England Vicar: "I'm for Prohibition, just against its enforcement."

> *The Roaring Twenties roared through Georgetown just like everywhere else. Numerous newspaper accounts throughout the decade report stills and smugglers operating from Little River to McClellanville and beyond. The region's small and winding inlets had served blockade runners well during the Civil War. They did the same for rum runners. The woods and swamps were wide and wild with an aroma that smelled like money to many... Georgetown had, over three or so centuries, developed a taste for the traditional bread and butter of any organized criminal cabal; namely drinking, gambling and impersonal sex. From the available record, it appears that local public officials either shared in some of these appetites or had a motive to look the other way while others sated themselves.* [41]

So, it was a teenage Alfred who one day found himself in the hands of law enforcement being returned to his father, John, and accused of "running shine" for one of the local distributors. No charges were pressed, but his dad, in keeping with the discipline of the times, beat him within an inch of his life, leaving a lifelong impression. Family folklore indicates it was the only time that Alfred ever was in the hands of the law for the rest of his life. As to the rest of the Lebanese families in Georgetown, they seemed to have loved their gambling and an evening cocktail as much as the rest of society.

A kinder story of Alfred's role in helping the family in its businesses is of the many trips to Florida to haul cases of freshly picked oranges to his dad's or uncle's grocery stores. These were trips in less than perfect cars and trucks on roads that could leave your guts in pieces. Fresh fruit was a major offering of the Lebanese merchants. Keeping them stocked was a family affair.

Fish House

Alfred would spend his days working in the mill and his early evenings a block from the house at one of Georgetown's beloved landmarks: The Fish House. Sitting on the Sampit River as it enters the Port of Georgetown is what today seems like an ancient edifice. The boat shed was the home of Cathou & Sons Fish House, where Rene Cathou cleaned, packaged and sold his world-famous caviar that came from the incredibly abundant sturgeon that filled the waters of the Winyah Bay for as long as anyone can remember. In 1880, South Carolina fishermen harvested 250,000 pounds of sturgeon. [17]

The 100-year-old Fish House is at the end of St. James Street, where Alfred lived for most of his adult life. In town, interviewing the locals, the men who gathered there at the end of each day were the stuff that legends are made of. Big, hardworking men, who fished the waters, worked the mills and did all the tough stuff that is the essence of every community, came to sit and drink and "tell lies." Only the walls know the stories. Alfred in his final days still loved to walk down the street, stop and reminisce about the thousands of hours spent with his pals in this lovable legacy. The Fish House still stands today, looking little different than it has over the past 100 years; ramshackle maybe, quaint, surely, but powerful with its dry dock still caring for fishing vessels and anachronistic with its railroad-style pulley system. For me, as I first entered it with my wife, Alfred's daughter Mary Lou, it felt somehow surreal in the best sense of the word… having a disorienting, hallucinatory quality of a dream. The Fish House was part of Alfred's fantastic, dream-like life.

Epilogue

There is an epilogue to the football story. During the summers, Alfred worked at the International Paper Mill to help support the family. There, he suffered a debilitating industrial accident that cost him his left foot and left him with a limp for life. He was a three "letter man" at his high school, excelling in football, track and baseball. He underwent years of treatment and terrible operations but ultimately his leg was amputated below the knee. Alfred, in his strong, quiet way just moved on. He never complained. Never looked back. He celebrated the life and family he so loved. He believed himself blessed.

He remained at International Paper and married the love of his life, Louise, and raised his three daughters and son in Georgetown. In the 20 years I knew him, the accident never came up and the limp was never an issue.

The most touching stories about Alfred come from his wife and kids and the extended Joseph family. There was never a bad word mentioned. When asked for the most poignant moment that his son Alfred had with his dad, he offered a particularly troubling time in his young married life. Alfred Jr.'s second son, Thomas, was born with a rare blood disease that would cause his body to lose all of its immunities almost every 30 days, putting his infant life at severe risk. A painful medical protocol of daily injections of an experimental drug was the only path to possible survival. During this one week, it seemed especially difficult and baby Thomas was in constant pain. The doctors told the parents to prepare for the worst. Parents and medical personnel all attempted to calm him and assuage the tears. When recounting the story to me on Thomas' 19th birthday while at the beach house in Pawleys Island in 2017, Alfred Jr., with tears in his eyes recounted the moment when Alfred Sr. walked into the hospital room. *Thomas was crying and unresponsive to any help from any of us. My dad walked into the room. Thomas saw him, smiled, raised his arms up to him and at least for a time, the tears subsided and relief was at hand.* Thomas at 19 is a proud member of the U.S. Army serving his country in Germany.

Everyone talks of Alfred's gentleness, kindness, love. The image I always have of him was that of the gentle giant. Alfred lived his entire life as a peaceful, humble, loving man, just like his father. The eulogy given by the pastor at the packed St. Mary's Church at his funeral said it simply, but well:

> *Alfred as we know was a simple man with a big heart that loved everyone and he was also well loved and respected. Alfred was a gentleman each and every day of his life.* [1]

I would only paraphrase that in the slightest, Alfred was a gentle man.

VIGNETTE: MARY LOUISE JOSEPH
A Love Story for the Ages
Alfred Paul Joseph, Sr.'s wife

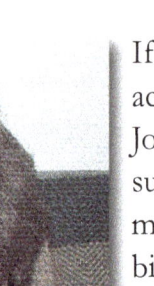

If the Lebanese family magic could be captured in a single action, it would have been the hug that took place at the old Joseph house on St. James Street one sunny afternoon in the summer of 2013. Two sisters, separated by a hundred or so miles and the frailty of old age, were reunited for one's 90th birthday. It was heart-warming, nothing short of chimera.

Picture a frail, 85-year-old Margaret Rose who had been house bound for much of the past five years, taking a three-hour car trip from Columbia to visit her sister, Louise, who was turning 90 this day. Rose, pushing her walker across grass and pavement, while the birthday "girl" paced the porch in eager anticipation. Cancer, shingles and a host of ailments had challenged the 85-year-old body in recent years, but nothing lessened her drive to be with her eldest sister on this memorable day.

No, Momma, stay here on the porch, she's coming up to you, came the direction from the protective daughter wanting to keep her mother from attempting the five steps to the sidewalk. *But I want to go hug her*. The wait seemed interminable. Three younger adults helped the 85-year-old on her trek, eventually discarding the walker for the triumphant climb up the steps. And then it happened!

It was a hug for the ages, Louise at 90, Margaret Rose at 85. It was reminiscent of that wonderful scene from "Romeo and Juliet" in the Zeffirelli movie. The two lovers hugged and kissed and wept as a sea of onlookers swirled about them. They noticed no one. They were reunited and the world stopped. One could hardly stand and the other could hardly stand still.

Maybe they both sensed this could be a last hug, but for those of us blessed to know them both, this was the type of hug they shared for the almost 100 years each had lived. Each reunion was as if it were the first and the last. The feelings were intense each time. The love never wavered. The mutual giving and caring and feeling never waned. We onlookers could only marvel in the moment and yearn for such intensity in our relationships.

This hug epitomizes this special family, a generation of people that helped move me to write their story.

It was only the opening scene in a very long celebration of the 90-year life, lived well, lived holy and shared by many. Soon the other octogenarian siblings would arrive – the soon-to-be 89-year-old brother Pete and the 84-year-old sister Christine. The quartet was now complete. The four, born back in the 1920s, were together again, and not for anyone's wedding or funeral, but to celebrate themselves. To revel in lives lived long and well. Their devotion to each other was profound. Even at their tender ages, two of the four were still driving and three of the four who lived in Georgetown would gather every Sunday for lunch at a restaurant that seemed as old as they were. Today's birthday feast and these Sunday lunches were remembrances of the grand feasts that took place every Sunday in earlier years at their parents' houses. Back then Sittee and Jeddi, the affectionate Lebanese names for the grandparents, in each of the families would host the meal in Georgetown or Kingstree with food abounding, kids everywhere and family as the binding force. Back then many of the families had eight or nine children and the feast was open to all… friends, families, visitors. The brother remarked "We have 350 years of siblings gathered here on the couch." The cameras and cameraphones began to pop.

A hallmark of the Lebanese is their love of good food and lots of it and their desire to share it. Today would be no exception. Twenty one folks would eventually sit for a dinner, but others would drop by to bring cakes and flowers and cards and gifts. Louise had children and grandchildren and nieces and nephews and cousins and friends who came. But this day seemed to be one for the ages and for those ageless octogenarians. This was no ordinary birthday, but this was how the Lebanese gathered.

A Very Special Family

The round dining table with four chairs was extended out to 16, a card table accommodated the others. A buffet table for the pork roast and flank steak and chicken and rice and casserole upon casserole was set. There were flowers everywhere. The red roses had to compete with the lilies and such a feast would not have been complete without the family priest and of course the blessing of the food with all holding hands. Three generations of the family and extended family were there, and it was a long and full day. Eventually the cakes and pies and the ice cream were brought out, and the combined revelers got to sing "Happy Birthday" to a beaming Louise.

But it was the endless hug that will never be forgotten, even in the recesses of old minds challenged with memory loss. July 23, 2013, will be forever etched in the hearts of those fortunate enough to be witness to this magic moment.

THE REMARKABLE INSTITUTION CALLED THOMAS'

For almost half a century, Thomas Café has been an integral part of the Georgetown business community, offering a rare combination of community fellowship and good food... it was like a second home to many Georgetonians through the years. Many yarns and memories exist about this café, which functioned for so many years as coffee houses of old. Here Georgetonians met to eat, relax and swap news items. If Thomas Café could talk, you would hear the most graphic and delightful account of Georgetown history, for this café has been a focal point of Georgetown life since Mr. E. C. and Miss Catherine first opened the doors in the depth of the Depression in 1933. There is something about Thomas' that is unique. It brought people from all walks of life together to share a joke and to laugh: to share the news, both happy and sad. It filled a unique role in the life of Georgetown and it will be missed. [20]

A single physical institution epitomizing the history of the Lebanese in Georgetown has survived almost the 100 years since making this port city their home. Thomas Café has the proud distinction of being the oldest extant commercial operation in this very old town to have been in continuous operation under the same family name. You could miss it if you drive through town too quickly, but you can't forget it if you ever stop and ask a local about it. It is a proud monument to my wife's maternal grandparents, Escie and Catherine Thomas.

Photo courtesy of Georgetown County Digital Library

Just steps from the Georgetown Clock Tower at the heart of town is a brick building sitting on the main thoroughfare, Front Street, and backing up to the Sampit River. At 703 Front Street is Thomas

Café. Two picture windows proudly announce the Thomas name and invite you in. Looking at pictures from 1905, the venerable building looks the same. The building once housed the general store owned by other Lebanese merchants at the turn of the century. Nicholas and Thomas Joseph ran N. Joseph and Brother, lived above the store and began to raise their families in this building. There's a sidewalk now, and electric street lights. But, the building is the same. It seems like the counter and tables and chairs and floor and ceiling are the same. The kitchen is pretty close to the same. In fact the refrigerator/cooler that sits behind the counter was purchased by the Thomas family used in 1956 and is still humming in 2017.

The fortunate part is that the venue is still intact. An editorial piece on the city, written by an out-of-town boater who often stopped in Georgetown on his family trips up and down the Intracoastal Waterway sets the Café in its proper historical context:

It's only got twenty chairs, six tables, six booths and eight stools, along the quintessential American counter. But it's got history and charm and love written all over it. It's open for breakfast and lunch, and there's no Sushi or tacos or anything that feels like a national food chain. This is a southern institution serving comfort food at its best and it has done it for over eighty years. This is eggs and country ham and grits and toast in the morning, and fried chicken and collards and red rice at lunch. There is no dinner served because that is when the proprietors were home taking care of the family and school and church.

There are the beautifully preserved historic landmarks to be seen, but then there are the surprises… like Thomas' Café. Just stepping through the doorway, sitting in the straight-back wood booths, and ordering a breakfast, for instance, allows you to view this mini-house-museum – a small town restaurant from the past, preserved for the NOW, because it was not new-improved artificially along the way. The collection of memorabilia about the Clemson Tigers is folk-art in the form of ceramic statues, clocks, calendars, door-push, swivel-stool-seats, etc., etc., etc. It has a simplistic beauty – an honest All-American charm… just as it is! The dinette sets in the front of the store, and an extra-large one in the back, apparently seats the continuous flow of business people who gather at this table in the early morning hours to take and share their recent over-night news over their "cuppa-coffee." Who died… who came. Who left… or WHAT happened! Bigger cities do not and cannot have such one-to-one contacts with people, because they are too big, but Georgetown can, because the size is just right. We like Georgetown because it is natural and unspoiled and has not yet "new-improved" itself with artificial facades, where neither residents or visitors feel themselves comfortable." [32]

It's difficult to know where to start and only vignettes can begin to capture the rich history of this quaint institution.

A Very Special Family

I often close my eyes and try to picture Thomas Café in 1933 when husband and wife, Escie and Catherine Thomas, first opened their doors. They were young immigrants who had come to a new country at the turn of the century over the treacherous Atlantic in steamships from Lebanon packed with hundreds of other Mediterranean and European souls fleeing civil wars and famine and untold hardship to seek the American dream. Son Pete would join them in running the Café when he returned from World War II. Escie, Catherine and Pete all were very different personalities and had very different styles of running the Café. Escie, gruff and tough and all business. Catherine, soft and welcoming and always attentive. Pete a wonderful blend of the two. This, after all, was a family affair. As Pete likes to put it, "Mama was the brain trust and the pie maker… she did everything." Catherine in classic deprecating manner retorted, "We shared it."

Escie Butros Thomas was born in Lebanon in 1898 and came to America as a young man around 1915. Escie, like so many other Lebanese immigrants was at heart, a merchant, a trader and loved good food. When he arrived at Ellis Island as a teenager, no one from the family or Lebanese community was there to meet him. For that reason, he was sent to the children's dorm at Ellis for several weeks, until a family member finally came to retrieve him. He and two cousins first opened a grocery store, until the cousins returned to Lebanon. To hear it told, Escie originally only served two things in the Café that bore his name – his famous beef stew and hot dogs – and they were both served through a take-out window. Later the specialties would be fried chicken and pork chops. Escie's son Pete Thomas told me that Escie was more interested in the poker games that he hosted in the back room and upstairs, but history seems to belie that. For, at some point, the take-out became a sit-down, the menu became classic Southern café fare, and the Thomases were off on a multi-generational, multi-decades long entrepreneurial venture and adventure. It was truly a family affair. Every family member was expected to pitch in, and so they did. There are wonderful stories in the *Georgetown Times* about Escie:

- When the newly hired editor of the *Georgetown Times* first arrived in town, he showed up at the Café and ordered a cup of coffee. But he only had a $20 bill and handed it to Escie *"who was manning the cash register like Teddy Roosevelt atop San Juan Hill. I expected a raised eyebrow, a disclaimer, a passing comment about the audacity of offering a $20 bill to pay for a five cent cup of coffee. Mr. E.C. had never seen me before but he let me have it full blast: "Boy, this is no bank. The bank's across the* *street. You go over there, change that thing and bring my nickel back, he bellowed. That was my introduction to Thomas Café and to Mr. E.C., who quickly commanded my respect."* [15]

- According to a story of October 18, 1978 *"eating wasn't the best part – entertainment was. E.C. always thought he had to put on a show for the fellows out there – some of his favorites like Chief Fred Nobles, Lewis Freeman, Louie Bodian and some of the others who habitually came to take up their places at the sacred back table near the kitchen door. Thomas had his own crop of carefully cultivated irascibility that never failed him and caused others to quake. E.C. hated for people to order hamburgers, Mrs. Thomas said, and when I'd put the orders in, he'd let fly with a torrent of language, cussing in Arabic and English and I'd come tearing back to get out of earshot but it was all a show. E. C. just wanted to see the men laugh; he wasn't really that chauvinistic at all. He just had his own pithy and incomparable brand of commentary."* [15]

- Son Pete told the story that his dad, like many men born in the early 1900s, loved to gamble. The Lebanese in Georgetown were legendary at it. Slot machines in the social clubs, pool halls around town and the big on-going poker game in the back of Thomas Café and upstairs. According to Pete, the game went on continuously, often through the night. One story has it that Escie lost the ownership of the Café one night and won it back the next. Apparently, at least one wife of a player was very displeased about the gambling and called Police Chief Nobles ten times, until he showed up at Thomas one night and arrested all the players and fingerprinted them all. No charges were ever filed, and rumor has it the game resumed.

Miss Catherine is a wonderful contrast in style to her husband Escie. On the day that Miss Catherine and Pete were closing the doors for the final serving together, the Café was packed with well-wishers. Mayor Doug Hinds presented the two of them with a silver tray, *expressing the love and appreciation of friends for the decades of service and home cooking, plus never-failing courtesy, warmth and cheerful welcome they found at Thomas'.* [15, p5]

It was Miss Catherine who was the people-facing end of the business. She was the warm greeter. She was the fastidious server guaranteeing a glass of water and order-taking quickly and efficiently. It was she who spotted the regulars as they came and often placed their regular orders, even before they were seated. She also was usually the friendly face at the register, leaving Escie to his kitchen and his entertainment of the boys.

People loved the banana cream and lemon pies (no fruit pies) and the vegetables, the fried fish and roast beef and stew, a medley of good down home cooking. [15] Many others remembered the sumptuous fried chicken and the savory pork chops.

Pete Thomas, at 89, was the living repository of the legend. He was veteran proud and had the tattoo from World War II to prove it. He was as much of an institution in town as the Café that bears his family name. Rattling around in his balding head were almost a hundred years of memories, where the Café was both the center of his life, as well as the center and life blood of the Thomas family and the city of Georgetown itself.

Pete, until his death in 2016, and a bunch of his 80+ year old buddies still gathered almost every day for coffee, maybe a biscuit and a chance to tell stories and reminisce. Oh, to be a fly on the wall for those confabs. These guys had seen and done it all. Built and run businesses that were at the heart of the town. Fought our wars. Survived our great depression. Coached our kids and fathered and raised a generation that was able to stand on their shoulders and live the American dream. Most of these guys didn't travel much other than in their uniforms and didn't stray far from what is good and right about America and found it all, right here in this little port city. They were all immigrants of one sort or another, and all worked hard and played hard to survive into their eighties and nineties.

A few stories may help to capture a day in the life of the Café and the Thomas family may have been like. One seems right out of Mayberry RFD. Escie and Catherine's granddaughter, Mary Louise, my wife, fondly reminisces about the daily deliveries that were made to the imposing building just two doors down from the café. The edifice today is the Clock Tower. In the 1800s, it was the site of the slave market and, in the early 1900s, it was the town jail. Remnants of both are still open for tourists to visit and consider the traumas of our earlier history. Deliveries from the Café were often made to

the jail for those "guests" in lock up. This was not the high security prison of today, with its barbed wire and surveillance tower. This was more like Dodge City or, yes, Mayberry, with the Sheriff placing an order for two lunches for the town drunk or bar fighters or some ne'er-do-well. They had to be fed, and Thomas was the answer. On one occasion, a dapper gentleman came in, ordered poached eggs to be done just so, demanded special attention, and when the bill came, told Escie to give it to city hall. It turned out, he was a guest of the jail next door.

The other constant reminiscence of folks in town was that Thomas' was truly a family affair, over three generations of service. Escie and Catherine, both immigrants from Lebanon started the café, but their children and grandchildren all took turns as waiters, waitresses, bussers and clean up. Of course, their son, Pete, upon returning from the Navy and World War II, became the stalwart, along with his mom, after Escie died. But, daughter, Louise Thomas Joseph has a place in the pantheon of why immigrant family businesses survive and thrive. Louise, the mother of four, had a full-time job, working for the Georgetown Department of Education. Her office was almost directly across the street from Thomas Café. The lunch business was always brisk and more help was always needed. Louise would rush from her school district job over to Thomas on her lunch break and wait on tables every day. This was not just a once in a while, but rather the rule, not the exception. For years, she was a constant part of the Thomas troop. To this day, at age 90, her meals are always a rush. She needed to be at Thomas Café. The family needed her help.

A Very Special Family

Folklore in town, supported by some pretty hard facts, is that the table in the back, near the kitchen, was the meeting place for the movers and shakers in town. It was here that the bankers, lawyers, judges, politicians and businessmen would come to eat, have many cups of coffee and run the town. I have found no other gathering place in town that seems to challenge this history. Every week day, at 10, the boys would gather. Deals would be cut. Cases would be resolved. Transactions would be sealed. Careers would be made and broken. The City of Georgetown was the County seat and home to its Court and its Land Evidence Records. So much of what takes place in a democracy and in a capitalist country takes place in and around the seat of political and legal power. Thomas Café was just a couple of blocks from those seats of power, the Court House and the City Hall. Many of the power brokers took their seat at the Thomas table to discuss outside those walls what was taking place. Senators Hollings and Thurmond, two powerhouses in the U.S. Senate for much of the 20th century, ate there.

This quintessential Café was the gathering place.

> *More news, gossip, jokes, sports predictions and general conversation (much of which would be unprintable) has been said over the "coffee table" in the rear than is printed or aired through our local media. The food is always tasty, and is served in a way that makes you feel at home and want to come back. I suspect that if Pete and Mrs. Thomas put a concealed tape recorder under the "coffee table" a few years ago, they could have retired long ago and live in the "lap of luxury" for many years from the royalties – the most lucrative income, however, would have come in the form of "hush money" not to play a certain portion of the tape. I think back a few years ago when Mr. Thomas lay sick and dying – their friends and relatives came in and operated the place for several days. I suspect not one of them would take any form of compensation, save the personal satisfaction of helping a friend or loved one in time of need and grief.* [45]

In 1985, Pete sold the Café and the new owners chose to keep operating it under the venerable Thomas name. More than 30 years have passed since he cooked his last meal, but for many, you would think it was yesterday. When he and his nieces and nephew are together the menu is front and center. The meals that were served by each one of them as they grew up, and each took turns as waiters, waitresses, cleaners and all around help, are as vivid in their minds and on their palates as if they just came home from their last shift. They seem to be able to smell the grease, taste the grits and revel in shared memories of hard work and great times.

In whatever the circumstances, even a stranger was made to feel at home and the manner of service was ever of "wanting to please" the customer. A business establishment, with a distinct personality of its own, Thomas Cafe has certainly best represented what America and the free enterprise system is all about. I am going to miss this wonderful place of business on my future visits to your dear, old town...I will miss it as I would miss the passing of a fond friend of many years. [19]

A final anecdote helps to capture how that "Greatest Generation" of World War II fame lived and loved. Pete was at home and a very early morning knock startled him awake as he slept on the couch down in the living room. In skivvies and no shirt, reminiscent he said of his days on board warships in the Pacific theatre, he answered the door. There stood another "old guy" with a big grin and an abrupt question: "Pete, don't you remember me?" Of course, he didn't, having not seen him over 60 years. "It's me, Jimmy, we were bunk mates in the Navy. You never stopped talking about Georgetown and Thomas' Café and how I had to come eat there. Well, here I am, a bit late, but ready to see if you lied about 'the best breakfast in the whole world.' Put on some pants and let's go." Pete was flabbergasted, but didn't hesitate for a minute. Off they went, sat in a booth that was as old as their friendship and shared a poignant moment that only those who served in a war together could do. They then went out front and smoked the cigarettes as they had done so often aboard ship. Pete died about a year later, but friends had reunited for one last time.

Pete lived to be 92 and, up till the day he died, he rooted for Clemson and the Dodgers, because everyone else in the family rooted for the Gamecocks and Yankees. He still lived in the grand old first brick house on Front Street that Escie and Catherine built back in the 1930s.

Thomas' Café is still open and serving, under different owners, and the legend and memories live on. A story in the state newspaper said it has the distinction of being the oldest café in the state, continuously operating to this day under the same name. Maybe someday we'll even have the recipes for their much sought after beef stew, lemon pies and host of fried foods.

VIGNETTE: DOLLY RAAD-AWKAR
21st Century Lebanese Immigrants in South Carolina

More than a hundred years after the four Raad/Joseph brothers came to South Carolina from their village in Lebaa, Lebanon, another Raad family member emigrated with her family. One of the more fascinating aspects was that this member of the family turned out to be the Goddaughter of my wife's grandfather, John Raad Joseph. When Dolly and her family came to America in 2001, one of the driving forces was better education for their teenage sons. Lebanon was once again plagued with religious tension and sectarian strife with the Palestinian Liberation Organization and Hamas in control of many segments of the country. Instructive of what life was like in Lebaa for the Raads and other families was captured in a *New York Times* story:

In the picturesque Maronite Christian village of Lebaa, east of Sidon, for example, an opportunistic cousin of the Raad family arranged for Palestinians to rent a country house belonging to the father of Dolly Raad, a 26-year-old executive of Middle East Airlines. Miss Raad said it was a deal made both in acquiescence to the occupiers and to the prospect of money, for the P.L.O. leaders had, by all accounts, a lot of money.

The Palestinians turned the house into a restaurant and casino, provoking complaints from neighbors about noise and an unsavory clientele. Then, about two years ago, they locked it up, abandoned it and stopped paying rent, Miss Raad explained. "We asked for it back. They said no."

Both Lebanese and Palestinians describe such outright theft as a common practice of the P.L.O. guerrillas. They often took things from shops without paying, Miss Raad and others complained. Youssef Alifreh, a young Palestinian resident of the Burj al Shemali camp, near Tyre, confirmed it. "Now we are happy because the armed P.L.O. left," he declared. "When somebody wanted to buy something, he would take it and not pay, and if someone would complain, he would shoot him." [43]

In 2006, Dolly Raad-Awkar became an Adjunct Professor at the College of Charleston teaching the Arabic language. She had come to America with a strong background in both business and academia. For many years in Lebanon she had been an executive with Middle East Airlines and had taught at the prestigious Universite Saint-Joseph in Beirut, Lebanon. The 12,000-student University was founded in 1875 by the Jesuits and is considered by many to be the finest in the country. Seven of Lebanon's Presidents had attended St. Josephs.

My wife and I were heading from Georgetown to Charleston in early 2013 for a day of appointments and fun. I had learned from Isaac family members in Georgetown that Dolly would be a great source of information on the Raad family. We did not know at that time of the strong connection between Dolly and my wife's grandfather.

In a wonderful turn of events, when I reached out to set up an appointment with Dolly at the College of Charleston, she said: "Instead, let's meet at my restaurant Leyla on King Street." What a terrific surprise! Dolly and her family had set up what the reviewers say is *"Charleston's premier Lebanese restaurant serving authentic Lebanese dishes in an elegant modern setting and a sophisticated atmosphere."* In 2017, it was awarded Best Restaurant in the state!

This meeting turned out to be the start of a fascinating family story. Dolly was not only a delight to interview but she and her family were classic 21st century global entrepreneurs. Dolly, in addition to her role at the College, was running multiple international businesses. With a brother in Columbia and other Lebanese family members, she had set up Khoury Oriental Rugs back in 2003. With her husband, she was running Advanced Services, USA, which is an importer of Gourmet Lebanese food, beer and wine. All this came after a decade as the Manager of Commercial Agreements for Lebanon's flag carrier airline Middle East Airlines.

Over lunch, Dolly shared with us stories of growing up in Lebaa and working in Beirut. When my wife explained who her parents were, it was then that more of the onion unfolded. Mary Lou's grandfather had traveled back to Lebaa to settle family-owned property issues in 1956. Dolly had just been born and the family asked Mary Lou's grandfather to become her Godfather in a Maronite Catholic baptism. This fact had been unknown to the American second and third generation Raad/Josephs for this past half century. In addition, it was during this meeting that we learned that Dolly's brother is married to my wife's mother's niece and lives in Columbia, South Carolina.

In typical immigrant family tradition, the restaurant was being run as a family affair. Over the next hour, Dolly introduced us to her husband, who was the manager and buyer, and her two sons who were waiters as they completed their education at the College of Charleston.

Here we were 100 or so years after the first Raads had arrived and set up their businesses in South Carolina and a new Raad and her family had come on the scene making their presence known as entrepreneurs and academics. The 21st century chapter in the Raad successful immigration history was being written.

EPILOGUE

A hundred years after Kahlil Gibran penned that open letter to the Lebanese Americans who, like him, emigrated from Mount Lebanon and the surrounding areas to America, it's November 4, 2015, and residents of the small seaport city of Georgetown, South Carolina, awoke to news of a newly elected town council.

Alfred Paul Joseph, Jr., the grandson of four immigrants from Lebanon, led the ticket of six candidates, winning bi-partisan and bi-racial support in an election where voter suppression was charged, and 100-year-old racial lines in the city were once again resurrected.

For this Lebanese family, this was a momentous election. Al's Lebanese ancestors came to this city just over 100 years ago with barely the shirts on their backs. In many ways, as the Middle East continues to destroy itself in civil, ethnic, religious wars, a Lebanese immigrant's grandson being freely elected confirms his ancestors' decision to come to America. The election is the culmination of the immigrant journey from poverty and turmoil and living on the outskirts of political society to becoming a critical political player in the city his family so loved.

Who knows, in the future, he may well become Georgetown's Mayor as this city tries to recover from a devastating fire, a thousand-year flood, and the closing of one of its two major manufacturing mills.

Alfred Paul Joseph is the grandson of John Raad Joseph. As the youngest of the four brothers who, like so many immigrants and refugees, abandoned all in their homeland of Lebanon and took a tumultuous journey to the "new world," Grandfather John's action in Georgetown during his years of living here had a direct and very positive impact on Al Joseph's campaign. His legacy, and that of his family, was a major factor in Al's victory. As Al walked from house to house in the various neighborhoods throughout the city, he received warm welcomes and open homes from so many who remembered his grandparents and had benefitted from their kindness and largesse. On various Sundays, he was introduced in the African American churches as a friend from a family whose caring actions always spoke louder than words.

An excerpt from a Letter to the Editor of the *Georgetown Times* by Donald Gilliard gives a real sense of what Al's family has meant to many in this small city:

> *Al Joseph and the Joseph family have a long history with the African-American community and with my own family, as well. My late grandmother Ernestine "Sweet" Gilliard worked as a cook for Thomas Café, which was then owned by Al's material grandparents. I saw firsthand how race relations played out during that tumultuous time of racial unrest as I watched those working black hands discipline the Gilliard and Joseph children the same without a hint of concern from either child's parents. There were times when our grandparents didn't have much money and would send us to the meat market owned Al's paternal grandparents on St. James Street with just a note; try going to the grocery store now with just a note and no money. I can go on and on about the Joseph family's relationship with the African-American community. I'm saying this because there is no doubt that Al Joseph is no stranger to the African-American community.* [24]

This book has tried to capture the wonder of the immigrant challenges and, in this case, great successes. Four hardworking brothers, along with other Lebanese men and women, made courageous decisions to leave their war torn homeland of Lebanon to travel thousands of miles to a virtually unknown fate. A week after the election in 2015, as my wife and I sat with Joseph family members in Columbia, Beirut was once again torn apart by terrorist bombs, adding a poignant reminder of why they left and how blessed we are to be living in the land of the free.

In order to do justice to their journey, I've provided background on the history of the proud and accomplished Lebanese. Clearly, their Phoenician heritage and their Mediterranean culture made them so committed to their Christianity, their families and, quickly, to their newly adopted county. There are tragic similarities between the civil wars in Lebanon and the United States, and how each would affect these four brothers. In one instance, the war would destroy their economy and leave them with little opportunity, and in the other, it would be the war and its post-war reconstruction that would lead to greater opportunity for the new immigrants. Geographically, their old and new homes were thousands of miles apart but quite similar in terms of climate and proximity to the ocean.

The role that family played in the lives of these Lebanese immigrants was quite interesting to me. Each of the four brothers married Lebanese women and remained married to them for life. Each had three or more children and a passel of grandchildren. One hundred and seventeen years after their arrival in this country, those family ties are just as strong as they were in 1900, when this saga all began. Reunions over the years have been attended by hundreds of the extended family members.

Each of the brothers was successful in the new world, and each raised children to build on the American dream. The Joseph family successes came despite severe challenges:

> *As aliens in a foreign land, the odds against their survival were formidable… And only those who recognized the courage and fortitude of these indomitable immigrants would have predicted the degree of achievement and prosperity their children and grandchildren would enjoy. The sources of their pride in their heritage were the very factors alienating them from American society – the richness of the Arabic language that American could not speak or even pronounce, the Eastern liturgies of their churches that were so unlike American churches, and the Arabic culture.* [48, p17-18]

A Final Vignette: July 4th at Jeddi's

It was a blistering hot, beautiful Independence Day in 2015 and it was so representative of the Raad/Joseph family ethos that it is worth retelling.

There on the porch at Pawleys Island, overlooking the breathtaking Atlantic were three of the Joseph family matriarchs: Helen Walsh at 94, Rosemary Joseph at 87 and Pauline Sottille at 85. Each had come to revel in one of the annual Joseph family gathering, this the annual July 4 soiree on the beach at Dr. Johnny Joseph's house. To be more precise it was at "Jeddi's summer home." This classic old beach house dating back to the 1960s had been the gathering place for as long as anyone could remember.

On this day, there were about 60 members of the family, from the 2nd generation matriarchs down to the 5th generation new born. It was the usual grand affair with food for days. Hugs all around and a chance to sit in the rockers on the screen porch and reminisce and catch up on the marriages and births and deaths that had occurred over the past year. It was an interesting mix of family and friends. Local and from all over the state.

The wonder for me was to be able to watch the special, genuine affection shown by the 3rd and 4th generation for the matriarchs. The bond was firm. The love was palpable. The respect was deep.

Here were 60 folks from 10 or 15 different families all reveling in the oneness of a great heritage spawned by four brothers who left their homes and families in Lebanon to start a new life here in America some 115 or so years earlier. Here was testimony to their risk, to their love of family and to their indomitable spirit. You could sense it in the smiles of Helen and Pauline and Rosemary and in the warmth of their welcoming to all who came.

As the vintage and new military planes soared across the sky in tribute to America on this Independence Day, what better memorial to its greatness than to witness what is great about being an American: the freedom to be a family, live where you want, work as you wish and worship your God in whatever way it suits you. This diverse group of 60 seemed a fitting microcosm of everything that is right about being an American on July 4.

ACKNOWLEDGMENTS

This book could never have been completed without the incredible support and help from my best friend, my wife Mary Lou. It is simultaneously devoted to her very special family and to her drive to get it completed which are so indicative of her love and dedication to that family. Whether that was editing, chasing down family facts or photos, or the much-needed cajoling over the six years that the book gestated, she was always there helping me. This book is as much hers as mine.

So many people contributed to this effort that I hesitate to name names for fear of forgetting anyone. Apologies in advance to those I missed. Many Joseph family members contributed either by writing vignettes, or interviews, or phone calls or photos. Special thanks goes out to family members: Paul Joseph, Helen Joseph Walsh, Zion Joseph, Arthur Joseph Sr. and Jr., Barbara Amman Dumm, Raad Joseph, Timothy Joseph, Michael and Lisa Walsh, Selma Dorian Davis, Helen Bou Karam, Dolly Raad, Vincent Sottile, Mary Soteille, Joseph Isaac, Martha Ann Isaac, Linda Miller, Carter Joseph, Margaret Joseph Koutrolakis and the many members of the David and Paul Joseph families who shared their photographs.

A special thanks to the four professionals who were so much a part of this effort: Julie Warren, digital librarian, and Heather Pelham, videographer, for traipsing all over the state to do video interviews and shoot photographs and for providing vintage photographs from the Georgetown County Public Library Digital Collection; and to my tireless editor, Linda Ketron, and magical photo editor, Anne Swift Malarich.

REFERENCES

1. _____. Alfred Joseph's Funeral Mass, 2001
2. _____. City of Georgetown, SC website, history section, 2017. http://cityofgeorgetownsc.com/history/
3. _____. "History of Catholics in Georgetown," St. Anthony Guild Newsletter, 1910. www.stmaryourladyofransom.com
4. _____. "History of Lebanon," Wikipedia, 2017. https://en.wikipedia.or/wiki/History_of_Lebanon
5. _____. "History of Lebanon," http://oldsite.mountlebanon.org/histeast.html
6. _____. "History of The Ottoman Empire," Wikipedia, 2017. https://en.wikipedia.org/wiki/History_of_the_Ottoman_Empire
7. _____. "History of 1860 Lebanon Civil War," Wikipedia, 2017. https://en.wikipedia.org/wiki/1860_Mount_Lebanon_civil_war
8. _____. Lebanese Baptist Convention, Wikipedia, 2017. https://en.wikipedia.org/wiki/Lebanese_Baptist_Convention
9. _____. "The Massacres of 1840-1860." http://www.tanbourit.com
10. _____. Obituary, Free Press, Legacy.com, April, 2010. http://www.legacy.com/obituaries/kinston/obituary.aspx?pid=131769924
11. _____. "The Scottish Rite of Freemasonry," 2017. https://scottishrite.org/about/history/
12. _____. "St. Mary Catholic Church, Summerton, SC," Church Handout, unpublished, 2014.
13. _____. "Summerton," Wikipedia, 2017. http://en.wikipedia.org/wiki/Clarendon_County,_South_Carolina
14. _____. "The Syrian World," The Syrian World, 1951.
15. _____. "Thomas Café," Editorial Page, Georgetown Times, 1978. http://www.southstrandnews.com/
16. _____. U.S. Census, U.S. Census Bureau, 1860. https://www.census.gov/history/www/through_the_decades/overview/1860.html

17. _____. Article on Winyah Bay; The Post and Courier, Jan. 23, 2015.

18. Boukarn, Helen Raad. "The One-Hundred-Year-Trip," unpublished, 2009.

19. Brockington, W. H. "Thomas Café," Letter to the Editor, Georgetown Times, 1978.

20. Davis, Tom. "Remarkable Institution Called Thomas Café," Op/Ed page, Georgetown Times, 1978. http://www.southstrandnews.com/

21. Dorion, Nellie J. *Nellie My Story*, 1994.

22. Faase, Father Albert. Letter to the Editor, Georgetown Times, 1979.

23. Gibran, Kahlil. "I Believe in You – Address to Young Americans of Syrian Origin," The Syrian World, 1905. http://www.alhewar.com/gibran_to_young_american.htm

24. Gilliard, Donald. "Joseph Family," Letter to the Editor, Georgetown Times, 2015. http://www.southstrandnews.com/

25. Henry, Geoffrey and Jenkins, Ellen. "2010 Historic District Survey." City of Georgetown Planning Dept., 2010. http://nationalregister.sc.gov/SurveyReports/HC22003.pdf

26. Hitti, Phillip. "Immigration History of Arab Americans," Arab American Historical Foundation, 2017. http://www.arabamericanhistory.org/archives/immigration-history-of-arab-americans/

27. Joseph, Victoria. "Opening Statement, First Family Reunion," unpublished, 1974.

28. Joseph, Victoria. "Joseph Family History," Handout at Joseph Family Reunion, 1977.

29. Joseph, Victoria. "Something About Our Heritage," unpublished, 1979.

30. Kayal, Philip. *Who's Who in Utica*: "Where the Blue-Eyed Saxon is Finding Himself in the Minority, The Syrian Lebanese in America," Utica Saturday Globe, 1917.

31. Kenny, John. Interview with Mary Lou Joseph Kenny, 2016.

32. Leman, Marianne and Eddie. "Impression of the City of Georgetown," Letter to the Editor, Georgetown Times, 1984. http://www.southstrandnews.com/

33. Lewis, E. Maness. *QB to BG, Quarterback to Brig. General*. Pritzker Military Museum, 2000. http://www.pritzkermilitary.org/explore/library/online-catalog/view/oclc/248049623

34. Madden, Father Richard. "History of the Catholics in Georgetown," www.stmaryourladyofransom.com

35. McAlister, Robert. *The Lumber Boom of Coastal South Carolina.* History Press, 2013.

36. Moses, John G. *The Lebanese in America.* Education Press, 1987.

37. Powell, William S. *The Encyclopedia of North Carolina*, University of North Carolina Press, 2006.

38. Prados, Alfred B. "Lebanon," Homeland Digital Security Library, Library of Congress, June 8, 2006. http://www.hsdl.org/?abstract&did=464480

39. Raad, Nizer Toufic. "Raad Family Union." http://raad.org/history/html

40. Rogers Jr., George C. *The History of Georgetown County.* Charleston: University of South Carolina Press, 1970.

41. Rubillo, Tom. "Prohibition in Georgetown," Georgetown Times, 2012. http://www.gtowntimes.com

42. Shadid, Anthony. *House of Stone: A Memoir of Home, Family, and a Lost Middle East*, Mariner Books, 2013.

43. Shipler, David K. "Lebanese Tell of Anguish of Living Under PLO," New York Times, July 25, 1982. http://www.nytimes.com/1982/07/25/world/lebanese-tell-of-anguish-of-living-under-the-plo.html?mcubz=3

44. Walsh, Michael and Lisa. "Personal Interview of Helen Walsh," unpublished, 2017.

45. Westbrook, Joe. "Thomas Café," Letter to the Editor, Georgetown Times, 1978. http://www.southstrandnews.com/

46. Whitaker, Elizabeth Virginia. "From the Social Margins to the Center: Lebanese Families Arrived in South Carolina Before 1959," Clemson University, 2006. http://tigerprints.clemson.edu/cgi/viewcontent.cgi?article+1006&content=all_theses

47. Williams, Talcott. *Genocide Studies*, Publisher? 1930. http://scholarcommons.usf.edu/cgi/viewcontent.cgi?article=1165&context=gsp

48. Zogby, James. *Taking Root, Bearing Fruit: The Ango-American Experience*, American Arab Anti-Defamation Committee, 1984.

www.ingramcontent.com/pod-product-compliance
Lightning Source LLC
Chambersburg PA
CBHW040002290426
43673CB00078B/336